HOW TO PYRAMID
SMALL BUSINESS VENTURES

Mark Stevens

Parker Publishing Company, Inc.

West Nyack, New York

Reward Edition . . . . . . September 1979

Originally published as

How to Pyramid Small Business Ventures into a Personal Fortune

Library of Congress Cataloging in Publication Data

Stevens, Mark
   How to pyramid small business ventures into a
personal fortune.

   Includes index
   1. Business. 2. Small business. 3. Success.
I. Title.
HF5386 S867   658'.022   77-3444

Printed in the United States of America

HOW THIS BOOK WILL HELP YOU

How to Pyramid Small Business Ventures into a Personal Fortune is the first book of its kind. The first book written especially for the average man and woman, detailing the step-by-step technique of pyramiding a small investment into a large personal fortune. Practiced by millionaires here and abroad, pyramiding has been proven time and again as the fastest route to personal wealth.

Never before has the system been revealed simply and clearly enough for the average person to put into practical use. Whether you're a working person eager to make it big on your own or an established businessman looking to triple your company's size, this book will get you started towards your goal today.

The beauty of the system is clear—You don't need more than a small initial investment, less than $500, to get started. The secret is learning to make the most of that initial amount. To make it multiply many times over as you build a personal fortune in less time than you ever thought possible.

This book tells you everything you need to know. Like how to pick the most lucrative fields. How to obtain and use free government research spelling out exactly where the dollars are and how they can be made. And you'll read about the single greatest formula for business success, used by virtually every great millionaire from Ford to Onassis—how to find a void and fill it. This is the first time the full formula has ever been revealed in print.

You'll also learn how to use the fabulous system of leveraging to build a good deal of your fortune on borrowed funds. Like the multi-millionaires, you'll use leveraging to increase the stakes and spread the risks. What you don't have of your own to invest, this book will show you how to borrow from others and make it work for you. You'll get names and places for contacting wealthy investors ready and waiting to invest in new ideas, products and services.

And this is one book that doesn't deal in theories. You get detailed case histories illustrating how average men and women have used these principles to amass tremendous personal wealth. The result is a step-by-step pattern for building your own fortune.

You'll learn, for example, how Arthur B., a former one-store merchant, parlayed past profits into a million-dollar chain. How he grew from a small-time shopkeeper into an aggressive giant buying out competitors left and right. You'll get in on Mr. B's technique of horizontal growth and you'll learn how to make it work for you.

And you'll discover how Arnold and Joan K. used securities markets to make them millionaires overnight. How this husband and wife team put their heads together and parlayed a simple idea into a hot new investment vehicle worth millions in stock alone. You'll learn how you too can use publicity and the securities markets to pyramid a small success into a fortune.

How to Pyramid Small Business Ventures into a Personal Fortune tells you all you need to know to finally get in on the big money. The book wastes no words—pulls no punches. It tells how to get started on a shoestring. Suggests investment ideas for less than $500. Tells when to sell out and how to strike again while the iron's hot. Explains how to trade up, using mail order to get fast growth on a limited investment. And explains in simple terms how to make sophisticated growth strategies work for you. How to buy out competitors and swallow up suppliers, earning big money at both ends of the spectrum.

You'll also learn how to spot and avoid the 25 most common mistakes—the reasons most ventures fail before reaching the top. Interviews with scores of readers of my syndicated column have clearly defined these mistakes, and knowing them will help you avoid the pitfalls others have fallen victim to. Success, after all, means knowing what to do and what to avoid doing.

And once you've made your first million, the book reveals little-known ways to secure and protect it. Like how to invest in big money motion picture productions capable of returning up to 50 times or more of your original investment. And how to get in on millionaire-club tax shelters.

Although names, places and dollar amounts cited in this book have been changed, all examples cited are based on similar or typical cases observed by or related to the author.

The techniques, strategies and suggestions and other information cited in this book are based on the author's professional experience, but do not imply any guarantee of commercial or financial success.

From A to Z this book reveals the secrets of fortune building. Buying *How to Pyramid Small Business Ventures into a Personal*

Fortune may well be the best small investment you've ever made. It may change your life.

Mark Stevens

TABLE OF CONTENTS

TAPPING THE MONEY MACHINES— KNOWING WHERE THE DOLLARS ARE:

Lucrative Ideas for Starting or Expanding Business Investments

Think of the ten wealthiest people you have ever heard of. You know the names: Rockefeller, Getty, Hughes—and maybe that guy in the next town with the big estate. The house everyone tries to peek at when they drive by.

And now think of what they all have in common. Millions or perhaps billions of dollars. Yes. Land, gracious mansions, enormous yachts, thoroughbred horses, cooks, servants and the finest foods in the world. Yes. Power, prestige, fame and the freedom to do with their days as they please. Yes. To sail around the globe. To sun by day and spend the nights dining under the stars or gambling in lavish casinos. In Jamaica, Monte Carlo or Rio. Yes to this too.

But what else have they in common? What single characteristic distinguishes the rich from the average working stiffs? From the millions who never seem to be able to get ahead of the game? From those who can never take a day off without worrying about the consequences?

The answer is simple: *They are all in business for themselves.*
Think about it. One owns a manufacturing company, another an
oil firm and still another deals in stocks and bonds. None are tied
to a regular salary that someone else sets—and someone else can
take away.

It's clear enough—you cannot get very rich working for a salary.
It is virtually impossible. First the taxes will kill you. Once Uncle
Sam takes his chunk you are left with less than half the amount
you started with. What's more, there's no opportunity for that
big killing thousands of successful entrepreneurs make every
day. When you are working for someone else there's no chance to
make that one big deal that will set you up for life.

A top executive of a large, well-known company, for example,
may pull down $200,000 a year. In most cases, it takes the in-
dividual executive most of his or her life to reach this point—and
after taxes the executive is left with only $100,000 or so. Not bad,
but far less than the kind of fortune you can make in business for
yourself.

Jess Z. recognized the limitations of a salaried position when he
was only 31. So he gave up his job as a salesman for a children's
clothing manufacturer and opened his own firm—Kid Klothes—
selling a competing line. By using the contacts he developed
while working for the other guy, Jess built a prosperous business
from meager beginnings in less than two years.

And in the first month of his third year he made the deal of a
lifetime. Convincing a buyer for the nation's largest chain that
Kid Klothes was the best children's wear line in the country, Jess
won over the biggest account in the business. On the first year's
order alone he made a personal profit of $411,000—and over the
years wrote more than $282 million in business with the chain.
But that first big killing was more money than Jess had made in

the ten years he had spent selling for others. By the fourth year in business for himself he was a millionaire.

Success stories like this are common, everyday happenings for the nation's entrepreneurs. For the men and women wise enough to go into business on their own. To get a piece of the action by sharing in America's enormous wealth.

The free enterprise system is our country's greatest asset. Nowhere else on earth does business and industry flourish with such boundless energy. America's commercial muscle is felt around the world, creating profit, jobs and opportunities for millions. Opportunities for all who are aggressive enough to take advantage of this great national resource. Opportunities for young and old, white and black, men and women.

You can get started building your personal fortune by working with the business system—by making your first investment as an independent entrepreneur. And you don't even have to quit your job to get the ball rolling. All you need is a good idea, a few hundred dollars and the determination to make yourself rich.

Pyramid Investing can help you make it all possible. This little-known technique has helped thousands of average working people (many of whom we'll read about in later chapters) parlay shoestring investments of less than $500 into multi-million dollar fortunes that made them rich for life. And it doesn't take forever to make this killing; many have done it in five years or less.

Whether you already own a small business or have always worked for others, Pyramid Investing can help you multiply your worth to many times its current value. The technique has been used successfully to expand small companies into corporate giants and to help those with no business holdings build commercial empires.

Pyramid Investing is designed to make you rich. The basic
system is simple enough. It shows you how to spot the best
money-making opportunities and how to use them for your own
advantage. How to start out small and parlay your earnings into
ever-larger business interests—ever-greater personal wealth.

The secret is "productive reinvesting." Rather than hoarding
early profits or spending the money frivolously, Pyramid Investors apply their earnings to a series of increasingly large
business ventures. The cream from each successful investment is
skimmed from the top and is used for even better money-making
opportunities.

Pyramid Investing capitalizes on early profits as a means of
building a large personal empire. Only by continuously reinvesting this seed money can the average person turn a few
hundred dollars into a fortune. Pyramid Investing demands that
you forgo the natural temptation to spend initial earnings—and
that you parlay this sum into an ever-larger amount. Generally,
Pyramid Investors reinvest five-sixths of their initial profits.

Pyramid Investors, after all, are not interested in making a few
thousand dollars and then going back to the "go-nowhere
routine" of a dull job or a dying business. You are out to make
enough cash to bankroll the rest of your days. To be rich and at
leisure, free to do as you please. For this you'll have to forsake
the early rewards and reinvest your profits into more and more
lucrative opportunities.

"Productive reinvesting"—the Pyramid Investor's trademark—
means investing for a fast and substantial return on your dollars.
To be successful at the system, you have to buy into fertile
ventures that can triple or quadruple your stake in a few years or
less. You cannot spend too much time milking one investment.
The strikes must be fast and highly rewarding. You'll need the

time and money to take advantage of the really big deals as they open up to you.

Use the following timetable as a guide for your initial investments:

$500 investment . . . . quadruple within six months
$2,000 investment . . . . quadruple within four months
$3,500 investment . . . . triple within three months
$5,000 investment . . . . triple within four months
$10,000 investment . . . . triple within sixteen months

What it all boils down to is picking and choosing the few ideal investment opportunities that make the fast scores possible. Unique is the key word here. To make Pyramid Investing work, you have to develop fresh and original business strategies. Nothing strange or scientific—just far enough ahead of the competition to keep the field for yourself in the beginning. To rack up big bucks before others get wind of a good thing and rush in to imitate you. That early lead is all you need to get in, clean up and get out before the crowds converge. That's the way Pyramid Investors operate.

You don't need a crystal ball or some magical formula to discover the thousands of lucrative opportunities awaiting Pyramid Investors. Some of the best bets are revealed in readily available research reports, public surveys and academic studies. All you have to do is get the right publications and learn how to use them.

Government census tracts, for example, contain more valuable business information than you could ever hope to discover with a staff of hundreds. Census reports tell you all you need to know about prevailing market conditions, consumer demand and business competition. They can show you where it is best to start a business, open a new branch or build a whole chain. It's all laid out for you in clear facts and figures.

Take the case of Burt G., an aggressive Connecticut entrepreneur who operated a local chauffeuring service. He used the first few thousand dollars profit he made to buy the patent rights to a new type of billiards game—Mini-Pool. This is a game designed for those who like billiards but don't have the room in their homes for a full-sized pool table.

After running off an initial production of 300 tables, Burt was ready to open a shop to sell the units. But where should he locate? Of all the available sites, which was the most promising?

Burt turned to the latest census reports (available at most public libraries) for the answer. Knowing that he wanted to stay in his home state, he searched for those parts of Connecticut with the greatest number of prime sales prospects. He knew his product would appeal mostly to apartment dwellers or owners of small homes—primarily middle-income consumers aged 15 to 40.

Census publications showed exactly where to look. The Census on Population and Housing, for example, provided the following types of data for all of the geographical areas in the state: population figures by sex, race and age; types of households; numbers of rooms per household; the presence of appliances; and the number of automobiles. Burt used this information to pinpoint the communities offering the greatest number of target consumers.

Burt turned to the Census on Business for a look at the available competitive data. Business census reports list retail and wholesale firms located near all of the sites Burt had under consideration. Each company is listed according to sales volume, number of employees and sales per merchandise line.

Coupled with consumer and population reports, the Business
Census provides entrepreneurs with a clear picture of target
communities. You know in advance if the residents and the
competition make the area a suitable place to launch new or
expanded businesses. It's the kind of data that helps you pick
out the choice money-making opportunities—to tap the most
lucrative markets.

In Burt's case all of the signs pointed to a busy mall in Stamford.
The site was convenient to six high-rise apartment complexes as
well as two developments of small, single-family homes. What's
more, consumers in the area were mostly young marrieds—
traditionally big spenders for games and other leisure products.

The planning was perfect. Acting on the census data, Burt
opened his first store in the busy mall—and it was an immediate
success. Local consumers loved Mini-Pool and purchased 211
sets the first month alone. At $190 per unit, Burt cleared sales of
more than $40,000 in less than four weeks of business.

And that was only the start. As word of the game spread, mail
and telephone orders poured in, and Burt opened two new retail
outlets in the first year. Exactly 14 months from his first sale,
Burt was sitting on one of the hottest new consumer items in the
country. All of the famous toy giants bid sky high for the
distribution rights, and leading department stores begged for all
of the shipments they could get. As a result, Burt's newly in-
corporated business was generating sales of close to $2 million—
profits exceeding $450,000.

"It probably never would have happened this way if I hadn't
picked the right location from the start," Burt says. "Unless you
know where to look for those really ripe opportunities, you can
get drowned in losses before you have a chance to make a dime.

Use census reports and other valuable government publications, and you'll get the head start that is so vital to success."

You too can make census data pay off. Be aware, however, that careful selection is the key to success. The Census Bureau publishes a wide range of reports from massive volumes on national and state statistics all the way down to tiny census tracts covering blocks of about 5,000 people each. Knowing what you want beforehand can help narrow the search.

Everything you need to know is contained in a helpful little pamphlet called the Bureau of Census Catalog. This invaluable guide lists all of the Bureau's publications, including a brief description and retail price for each. You can get your copy by writing to the Superintendent of Documents, Washington, D.C. 20402.

While you are writing, don't limit yourself to the Census Bureau. Helpful as this agency is, there are literally scores of other government departments ready and willing to divulge valuable data. Where will the new roads be built? What new products does the government want to buy? When will bids be announced for small business contracts? Will new business loan programs be established? Is the state selling off real estate at auction?

You can be privy to news of these developments by keeping tabs on the whole gamut of government departments. It's a lot easier than you may think. Just thumb through the local telephone book for the names and addresses of federal, state and local government agencies. Write to each, requesting inclusion on their mailing lists. It's that simple. You'll receive press releases, topical announcements, official reports—and more. Get on the General Services Administration list, for example, and you'll be invited to bid on thousands of government contracts. Who knows, you may start off small and grow to become one of Uncle Sam's big suppliers.

Best of all, cultivating government sources assures that you'll get advance information—and that's the best way to make Pyramid Investing work for you.

Another good idea is to hook up with a powerful trade association as soon as you get started as a Pyramid Investor. Trade groups can give you the power, prestige and inside information generally unavailable to independent entrepreneurs.

Typical trade groups are non-profit organizations representing member companies in a single field or industry. The purpose is to achieve power through numbers—to work together for common goals and objectives. To share knowledge, influence and technology.

As an individual investor operating in our complex economy, you are a little fish in a big pond. You have very little influence with the powers that be—local, state or federal. So if you need a zoning change or a political favor to pull off a big deal, you don't have much chance of getting it on your own. For this reason, some of the best opportunities may slip right through your fingers.

That is why trade associations make so much sense for Pyramid Investors. By joining with a group of your fellow entrepreneurs, your single voice becomes a chorus. You suddenly have friends and allies in high places. And since there is power in numbers, your business interests assume equal significance with those of giant corporations. You'll need this edge when it comes to finding and capitalizing on the real money-making opportunities.

What's more, trade groups provide you with all of the services available to large corporations at a fraction of the going costs. Most offer a full range of business aids including news publications, technical assistance and management training.

While the expense for this help would be prohibitive on an individual basis, the cooperative nature of trade groups lets you enjoy these competitive benefits at a price you can afford. Membership fees will generally average less than one percent of your expected annual sales.

Trade organizations help you spot the most lucrative opportunities—and capitalize on them—by offering the following services.

Information Exchange: Staff communication experts pass on to you news of the latest trends, technical data, research studies and legal developments. They serve as your eyes and ears to the world, collecting and condensing the data you need to be effective in our fast-paced economy.

The method of transmitting membership data depends on the size, budget and operating style of each trade group. Some prefer to publish single-item reports, and others issue regular newsletters covering a wide range of activities. Although the more elaborate publications may require extra subscription fees, the extra expense is usually a worthy investment. No other periodicals speak so directly to your special business interests. They can tell you precisely where the real money is being made in your field or industry. And as a Pyramid Investor, that's what you need to know.

Finally, some trade groups prefer to communicate on a personal level through seminars, conferences and private meetings. It is a good idea to attend as many of these events as possible. There is no better way to find out what's happening in the industry than to sit down and talk with fellow investors.

Public and Government Relations: The trade association also serves as your public relations arm. Association executives maintain close relationships with government agencies, the news media and public interest groups. The idea is to keep these powerful forces up to date on your thinking. Do you favor local tax cuts? Should there be a new sales tax? Should government promote or curb imports? Trade groups let the leaders know where you stand!

Trade groups also maintain ties with government leaders in order to bring about changes in existing legislation. Politicians, bureaucrats and the like are barraged with studies, research reports and opinion surveys showing why certain laws and regulations are unfair to you and your industry. These aggressive activities often produce the desired end: Legislation which prevents you from making sound investments is dropped or amended. You are free to move in and take advantage of the ripest opportunities.

Technical Services: You can also turn to trade groups for expert technical aid. Let's say you read in the association newsletter about a simple new technology that can cut your production costs in half. If you have trouble putting the new system to practical use, the association may send along a staff expert to help you out.

This kind of personalized assistance is usually free to members and should be fully utilized whenever the need arises. After all, the true value of your trade association is its rich diversity of functions and services. Feel free to use each and every one of them. They can help you make the most of your Pyramid Investments.

Trade services certainly helped Bud J. of Albuquerque, New Mexico. Bud's trade association, in fact, helped put him on the map as the biggest, richest and most powerful land speculator in the southwest.

It all started when Bud—a former bus driver—began thinking of
buying a small piece of property he passed every day on the bus
route. It was just a sandy lot located off the main highway, but
Bud thought it had potential. A new hotel was going up about a
mile away, and Bud thought his site would be perfect for a gas
station. So he took a chance, withdrew $1,600 in savings and
bought the lot.

As a landowner—albeit a small one—Bud decided to join the
state association of real estate investors. It was a wise and
profitable move. This middle-aged bus driver, who previously
knew little if anything about real estate, got all the education he
ever needed at the trade group's very first meeting. Taking him
for one of their own, the members confided in Bud that a
mammoth *Fortune* 500 company was thinking of buying up large
tracts of mineral-rich land in the middle part of the state. Word
had it that the company would pay premium prices for the right
parcels.

That was all Bud had to hear. He knew it was the opportunity of
a lifetime. The chance to leave the endless boredom of the bus
route and to make the kind of big money he always dreamed of.

Bud knew he had to act fast to buy up some of the speculative
land before the big mineral company moved in. But first he
needed money. So he asked an executive of the real estate
association to help him sell the small lot he'd purchased six
months before. As it turned out, a buyer was easy to find.

The motel nearby was now completed, and Bud's lot was indeed
ideal for a service station. Bud's contact at the trade association
put out feelers with the major oil companies, and soon they were
all bidding for the property. After watching the price climb
steadily for two weeks, Bud sold the site for $73,200—a profit of
more than $70,000 after property taxes.

Now he had cash for the big deals. Like a true Pyramid Investor, Bud turned right around and put his new-found capital to work. He bought 700 acres of the speculative land he'd heard about at the trade meeting. The price: $100 per acre.

Now all he could do was wait. Wait to see if the big mineral company from New York would move in and start buying up the land for exploration. Bud was confident—and as it turned out, he had every right to be.

One hot day in August two top executives from the New York conglomerate landed at the Albuquerque airport in a sleek private jet, boarded a limousine into town, walked into the county clerk's office and registered their company's intention to purchase 142,000 acres of land south of the city. Initial tests proved the land was mineral-rich, and the company was willing to pay dearly for its acquisition.

Local landowners knew they could hold out for top prices—and they did. The trade association became a focal point for their collective action, and they presented a united front to the corporate buyers. As a result, no one sold out cheap.

When the bidding and waiting game was over, the mineral company agreed to pay $3,125 per acre—a fabulous sum and a fantastic victory for the landowners. For Bud J. the day of great wealth had arrived. His 700 acres brought $2,187,500 and made him a multi-millionaire overnight. And this was only the beginning. Bud never let up on his Pyramid strategy. He formed the B.J. Real Estate Investment Company and bought and sold huge tracts of land in New Mexico, Nevada and Southern California.

He was soon the largest owner in the southwest, employed 116 real estate salesmen, and lived on a personal estate of 212 acres.

And he credited it all to that first tidbit of information he picked up at the trade group meeting. The information that made it possible for a middle-aged bus driver to strike it rich in the prime of his life.

Luck obviously played a part in Bud's success story. But before the fates started looking his way, Bud was smart enough to buy that first piece of property. He was smart enough to spot a money-making opportunity and aggressive enough to act on his hunch.

That's what Pyramid Investing is all about. Since you can't always rely on luck, we offer a better way. Rely on yourself. Rely on your own instinctive abilities. Trust in the knowledge that you too can pyramid small business investments into a personal fortune.

All you have to do is practice the techniques outlined in this book. And think positively. Know that you don't have to be born rich—you can make yourself so. Recognize that the greatest stumbling block to acquiring wealth is simply a "mental block." It's that self-defeating notion that average people like yourself can never be counted among the moneyed classes.

That's pure nonsense. Thousands of men and women have soared from low- and middle-class backgrounds to astronomical wealth. Take the original Fords and Rockefellers. Both were working men who became billionaires. And success stories of recent years are just as dramatic. A poor boy from Brooklyn, New York, for example, turned a new investment idea into a billion dollar, multi-national empire overnight. He is now, in his forties, one of the richest men in the world.

Once you know that you too can acquire great wealth and status, you will assume that all-important confidence so crucial to the

Pyramid Investor. For the first time, you will open your eyes to the money-making opportunities all around you. You will, above all else, learn how to "find a void and fill it."

This simple-sounding directive is actually the real secret behind every modern commercial success the world has known. From the Volkswagon automobile to *Playboy* magazine. From Hugh Hefner to Howard Hughes. All have filled a void in the market-place. All have provided a popular product or service not previously available from any other source

That, in a nutshell, is the secret of acquiring wealth. Look for those voids—and fill them. You don't have to come up with anything as complex as an automobile to do it. Just think of how much money has been made on the simple can opener. Billions.

New opportunities are opening up all the time. And that's the real beauty of it—there are always new angles to play, new ways to strike it rich. Take the hottest consumer product on the market today: the slow cooker. Women are gobbling them up by the millions because the product satisfies the new emphasis on freeing women from kitchen work. If you had simply presented this idea to a manufacturer you might well be into your second million by now.

So you see you don't have to be a great scientist, philosopher or engineer to spot the voids and fill them. Just read the newspapers. Talk to your friends and neighbors. Ask what bothers them, what would make their lives easier. Keep up with the trends and patterns of modern life. Remember, we live in a fluid age, and every change in lifestyles brings about new demands for products and services.

Be sure of one thing. Next week, next month, next year and into the next decade—thousands of people just like you will come up with million-dollar ideas to make them rich. They'll probably start small, build on success and parlay their winnings into a fortune. They'll come up with new inventions, contraptions or services. Or perhaps they'll just buy that right piece of property in the right place at the right time.

However they do it, they'll all share a common experience—they'll find a void and fill it. Why not do the same? Start today. The sooner you start, the sooner your chances of being rich. Do it!

BEHIND THE LITTLE-KNOWN
TECHNIQUE OF PYRAMIDING:
Learning the Secret
to Geometric Growth

2

Let's take first things first: money, money, money. Although you're not going anywhere unless you have some, don't be discouraged if your pockets are empty. There's no rule stating that you have to make a fortune with your own resources.

If you've never bothered to save—or if your funds are tied up in a go-nowhere business—then just turn around and borrow the money you need from others. There's always someone willing to take a stake in a new business venture. Just offer them interest in return—or even better, offer a share of the "action" once the profits start rolling in. That should be ample inducement for even the tightest creditor.

If you need $500 to make your first Pyramid Investment, for example, and you only have $300 in savings, borrow the balance from a bank or finance company. Do the same if you are lucky enough to have $85,000 and need $50,000 more to expand a going business. In either case, the interest charges are tax deductible and are well worth the expense. After all, the funds are being used to build your personal fortune.

The two major types of loans are intermediate (one to five years) and long term (five to twenty years). To secure either type, you'll usually have to show projected earnings great enough to repay the loan within the specified time. That's usually no problem if you have a promising business or if you're working with a hot new idea.

Once you've made a decision to borrow, check out the various lenders. Shop around for those most suitable to your company's needs. You'll probably have the best luck securing one of the following types of loans.

Small Business Administration Loans: The SBA is the federal agency most active in the wide range of small business affairs. This is especially true when it comes to financial assistance. No other agency can hold a match to SBA activities.

The SBA makes both intermediate- and long-term small business loans at modest interest rates. Independent entrepreneurs may borrow up to $350,000 in regular business loans directly from the SBA or may participate in SBA-guaranteed bank loans. Contact your nearest SBA field office (located in major cities) or write the Small Business Administration, Washington, D.C. 20416.

Small Business Investment Company Loans: SBICs are licensed and regulated by the SBA and function solely to provide small businesses with equity capital and debt financing. SBICs will help you meet your cash requirements by any one of the following arrangements:

- purchasing debentures issued by your company
- purchasing capital stock in your company
- making long-term business loans
- purchasing debt securities

For more information on SBIC financing write the National Association of Small Business Investment Companies, 1441 L. Street, Washington, D.C. 20416.

Mortgage Loans: You can use your mortgageable property as security for long-term loans from commercial banks, savings and loan associations and insurance companies. If loans are granted, creditors generally retain liens on the properties. Compare the interest rates and other terms offered by the various lenders before making a final decision. Keep in mind that you will pay higher interest rates for standard bank loans than for SBA- or SBIC-sponsored financing. Checking out these sources is therefore a good idea before you go the commercial bank route.

Supplier Loans: You may also be able to arrange low-cost loans through current or prospective suppliers. Manufacturers or wholesalers may be willing to lend you money if you've come up with a winning idea to help them move goods. Remember, when going after this kind of loan, direct your pitch to the supplier's self-interest. Show him how he can benefit by your success—and you may get the needed funds.

Life Insurance Company Loans: Providing you have some form of collateral, life insurance companies may be willing to lend you money for business ventures. This is important, because these loans may be arranged for longer periods than commercial bank loans. So check with insurance companies if you need money you can pay back over an extended period.

Property Sale and Lease-Back: If you are already running a business, you may find that most of your capital is tied up in fixed assets such as plants, warehouses and store facilities. That means there's little cash on hand to fuel your next Pyramid Investments. You simply have no way to make your business grow.

Have faith, however, for there is a solution. You may sell your buildings or other real property to insurance or finance companies and then lease back the assets over a period of years. The sale provides you with a cash lump sum for making your next Pyramid Investment. The arrangement frees substantial capital for use in operating ventures.

Wherever you look for money, be sure to approach the borrowing process with a specific plan. It's important to know beforehand just how much capital you'll need to satisfy long- and short-term investment objectives. Establish a plan and stick to it. The same degree of caution exercised in personal financial management must be applied to all business borrowing.

Elton I. of Providence, Rhode Island borrowed money only when he needed it. And that was a full two years after his initial Pyramid Investment of $411 in a small card shop proved extremely successful. In that time, Elton's store, Main Cards and Novelties, tripled in size and soared in sales to ten times its initial volume. Once annual sales pushed beyond the quarter million dollar mark, Elton decided to sell out and move up. It was time to take his merchandising talent to the big leagues.

For Elton, that meant only one thing—setting up his own full-fledged department store in the city's main business district. He was confident that his policy of cut-rate prices and superior customer service would succeed where other stores had failed.

And he knew it would take the volume of a full-sized department store to make the kind of fortune he had his sights set on.

So he went ahead with plans to buy and convert a vacant building that seemed just right for the new venture. He met with a broker, hired an architect and started arranging for merchandise shipments. But just as everything seemed to be flowing along without a hitch, a problem developed. Renovation costs ran ahead of projections, and Elton found himself short of funds to finish the job.

The solution: Elton turned to the Small Business Administration for an emergency loan of $51,000. He chose the SBA because he believed the agency was most sensitive to small business needs and because he wanted to get the lowest interest rate possible. He made a wise choice. Thanks to a little help from a local Congressman, Elton obtained his loan in record time. He was able to put the finishing touches on his beautifully remodeled $1.4 million store and to open the doors to the public on schedule.

On opening day alone, Elton's Emporium rang up sales of $70,312—about $20,000 more than the full amount of the loan. That, in a nutshell, is the beauty of business borrowing. The lesson is simple: When you don't have the funds to make Pyramid Investments, let others put up the money for you. If your idea is good, you'll be paying back the loans in no time at all.

Even if you are a poor credit risk, you can still raise the money for that first Pyramid Investment. Let's say you have no business experience, no collateral and no money of your own to put up. Don't despair. There's always someone willing to lend you cash if you can prove it's in their own self-interest to do so.

You'll probably have no luck at banks, finance companies or government agencies—but don't be discouraged. These established loan sources are well known for their overly cautious policies. They'll be of more value to you once you've established a sound credit rating.

Until then you can always turn to friends, neighbors, relatives or co-workers. Chances are you already know 10, 20 or maybe 30 people with money to spare to lend you enough for your first Pyramid Investment. After all, you only need $500 or less.

There's one simple trick to getting the cash: Be convincing. How do you do that? Just make the person feel that he or she will profit by lending you money. If you play your cards right, you won't even have to ask for the loan. People will ask you for a share of the action.

Here's how you do it.

- Think up a name for your new company.

- Type up a one-page summary of why the company is bound to succeed. Include an estimate of the firm's ultimate profit potential.

- Approach a potential loan source. Say you are starting a new company (mention the name) that you believe will make you very rich.

- When the person asks about your plans, request that everything be kept in strict confidence.

- Show the person your typed summary and answer all questions they may ask honestly and completely.

- If your business idea is as good as you think, the prospect will probably ask for a chance to invest in the venture. If so, you have your loan and are on your way.

- Sometimes, you may have to prod the person into acting. This can be done by asking the individual to invest in your venture in return for a share of the profits. Instead of paying interest on the loan, offer to reward the person with 10 percent of the first $10,000 profits; 5 percent of the first $100,000 and 2 ½ percent of the profits above $100,000. (These payments are for the first year alone.)

Profit sharing offers are a good way to generate business loans. As the borrower, you benefit in several ways. You get the cash for your business investments, and you don't have to pay interest on the loans. Since the lender shares only in the profits, you don't have to pay out anything until the business is a success.

When Lee S. decided to sell the work of local artists from her home in Providence, Rhode Island, she needed $350 to buy displays, stationery and promotional posters. Having once gone through bankruptcy proceedings, however, Lee found it impossible to borrow money from banks or other private sources. As far as "the establishment" was concerned, Lee was an unacceptable credit risk.

So she did the next best thing. She drew up a description of her business plan, including a list of reasons why she believed it would succeed. The idea was a good one—and she presented it clearly and honestly to a co-worker at a furniture plant where they worked. The friend was eager to participate and came to work the next day with the full $350 in cash.

Lee's idea was a winner—and both women fared very well indeed. The plan to sell original oil paintings direct from Lee's home met with widespread popularity from the start. The appeal was two-fold. First, the work was done by local artists—all friends and neighbors in the community. Second, the works were sold at the lowest possible prices. By eliminating the expense of renting and renovating an elaborate gallery, Lee was able to offer exceptional values on all of the works up for sale.

Working at home only on evenings and weekends, Lee managed to sell 611 paintings in the first year of operation. At an average price of $95 per canvas, the total take came to $58,045. Subtracting all costs, including her co-worker's share of the profits, Lee cleared $31,002—four times her yearly salary at the furniture plant.

Lee's very first year as a Pyramid Investor was a productive one. She earned enough to quit her dull job, to put money in the bank for the first time in years and to treat herself to a royal blue Cadillac.

And most important, she did it all on borrowed money. She used "leverage" to get her start in the business world. A single loan got Lee's foot in the door and started her on the road to personal wealth.

As it happened, it didn't take Lee long to rise to the very top. One of her best customers—a wealthy plastic surgeon—believed Lee's shop-at-home idea would make an excellent investment opportunity. He wanted a piece of the action and offered to put up $100,000 to franchise the system nationally.

The two formed a corporation and set up a sales agency almost immediately. The appeal was simple. In return for a $5,000 fee, the corporation, Home Galleries, Inc., would license franchisees to set up the patented at-home art shops. In addition to the initial fee, franchisees agreed to buy all paintings direct from Home Galleries. The partners stood to make a bundle at both ends by this arrangement.

In three years time, the firm rewarded the partners well. The two were married and became millionaires many times over.

Presiding over 671 franchises in 14 countries, they raked in fees totalling more than $3 ½ million. Add to this their cut on the sale of paintings, and you're talking about an annual income of close to $7 million.

You could say Lee's first loan was her passport to the upper class. Her ticket out of the grimy factory—away from the drudge work she'd done all her life. She was now rich, free and independent—and she owed it all to leverage. She owed it all to that first business venture she'd launched with someone else's money. Let that be a lesson to you. Remember, if you have the will to get started on the road to wealth—you'll find the way to do it.

Another important lesson can be found in the way Lee handled her money. Unlike many newly successful investors, Lee never lost control when the money started flowing in. She always treated her earnings with intelligence, using some for personal luxuries but putting aside the bulk for her next Pyramid Investment. And when it comes to amassing a personal fortune, that's one of the real keys to success. You have to learn to "parlay" your profits—to strike a balance between present income and future growth.

Spending as much as you make as soon as you make it defeats the whole concept of Pyramid Investing. Pyramid Investors have one goal: to be super rich. We don't believe in achieving mild success, cashing in our chips and stopping there. No. We believe in going all the way to the top. To the wealthy classes. To that special status in life where you never have to work, sweat or worry about money again. Where time is yours and you have nothing to do but enjoy it.

We believe in going all the way because we know it can be done. We know you can do it. And it's easier once you've made your first Pyramid Investment. Once you've started the ball rolling and have savored that first taste of success, you know you can go all the way. Your momentum is established. All you have to do is map your strategy carefully, and you'll make that first million. It doesn't make sense to settle for less.

How, you may ask, do you balance income between present needs and future growth? How do you live off your earnings while simultaneously putting aside enough for the next Pyramid Investment? Well, if you've ever managed even the simplest family budget, you know the answer: Live below your means. You simply have to put off living the high life until you've reached the apex of the pyramid.

When it comes to Pyramid Investing, patience is a virtue. You have to wait to spend big until after you score big. That's the only way to be sure you'll have enough cash on hand to make increasingly large and more profitable Pyramid Investments.

That's not to say you have to live from hand to mouth until you reach the top. Far from it. Chances are your standard of living as even a novice Pyramid Investor will be many times more lavish than your previous way of life. More money, more power, more freedom and more personal status. You'll be your own boss from the very first day—and you'll be on your way to building a personal fortune. If you have to wait awhile before indulging your every whim—so what. In a few years you may have more cash than you could ever hope to spend. The Pyramid Investing cash machine may fill your coffers faster than you can empty them.

Just how should you divide business income between present needs and future growth? How much of your early profits should you put aside to parlay into even greater sums? Although your strategy may vary somewhat according to personal considerations, use the following chart as an investment guide.

Business Investment Number:	Percentage of Earnings to Spend:	Percentage of Earnings to Reinvest:
I	25%	75%
II	30%	70%
III	38%	62%
IV	51%	49%
V	85%	15%

Three important points must be stressed here. First, you will notice that a very small percentage of your first investment's earnings may be spent—only 25 percent. If that's not enough to live on comfortably, keep your job or other source of income going until the earnings start flowing in from Investment II. By this time, the profits should be substantial enough for you to afford a comfortable standard of living even though you'll be spending only 30 percent of the total earnings.

Second, note that by the fifth investment you need save only 15 percent of your earnings. That's because savings are no longer crucial to you. Since you are already at the Super Investment stage, there's no need to amass money for the next venture. You have reached the top of the pyramid. Your fortune is in the millions, and you can afford to spend every penny of your enormous earnings on personal luxuries. We recommend that you continue to save 15 percent of your earnings just to add to your sizable nest egg. You can at this point, however, do as you wish. As you please. It's a privilege of wealth.

Third, you may achieve the 85 percent spend category before your fifth investment. If, as often happens, your second or third business venture proves to be a gold mine, you can start living like royalty right away. No matter how much time has passed and no matter what stage of the investment cycle you've reached, once your earnings reach into the millions you have arrived as a successful Pyramid Investor. It can take weeks, months or years—but when it happens you can lavish on yourself every luxury you've ever dreamed of.

Cheryl F.'s experience shows how Pyramid Investing can take you from near-zero assets and a dead-end job to a position of great wealth and power—to the top of the business world—in less than a year. Although the case is unusual for its rapid success, Pyramid Investing does make it possible to achieve a meteoric ascent from rags to riches.

Cheryl's greatest asset was her inventiveness. She knew that to be a success she would have to "find a void and fill it." She knew she'd have to come up with a product or service with great potential demand but little existing competition.

And then she hit on just the thing. As the assistant to a well-known New York veterinarian, Cheryl dealt with thousands of wealthy animal-owners living in and around Manhattan's so-called "silk stocking district." Over the years she heard the same request time and again: "Find us a luxury boarding kennel that will care for our dogs and cats while we are abroad or are off for a weekend at the shore. A kennel that will treat our pampered pets in the style they're accustomed to. That means air conditioning, soft beds, special diets and daily baths. We don't care how much it costs. Money is no object."

After years of telling clients that no such place existed, Cheryl finally realized she was turning her back on a fortune.

"Those wealthy New Yorkers had nothing but money to burn," Cheryl says, "and I was determined to help them spend it. So I opened up a luxury boarding kennel and took the business myself."

Until the opening of Cheryl's Hound's Haven, most boarding kennels were pretty much the same: dull, drab and dirty. All were a far cry from the magnificent penthouse suites many of New York's pampered cats and dogs were used to.

"I worked out a deal with a man who owned a little kennel on a choice block on Manhattan's fashionable upper east side," Cheryl explains. "He agreed to foot the bill for remodeling if I supplied the customers from my list of contacts. We shook hands and formed a partnership.

"I put up only $275 for printed invitations to announce our grand opening. My partner, on the other hand, spent $36,901 transforming his once plain little kennel into a pet palace. We offered individual 6 x 9 rooms, climate control units, 24-hour veterinary service on the premises, organic pet shampoos and even a pet psychologist. I don't know if the pets liked all the fuss, but the owners—the ones with the checkbooks—they ate it up. We were booked solid from the day we opened."

Hound's Haven proved extremely profitable. Considering the wealthy clientele patronizing the facility, Cheryl set the prices high—very high. Just like an exclusive resort for humans, everything at Hound's Haven was a la carte:

Daily boarding fee	$31
Meals	$11 each
Shampoo	$20
Pet Manicure	$18
Grooming and styling	$35

At these prices, it didn't take long to get the money rolling in by the thousands. The typical pet bill for a four-day weekend exceeded $350. And since Cheryl's was the only pet hotel of its kind around, she had more business than she could handle.

In just three months, Hound's Haven generated sales of
$130,000—enough to cover the initial investments and to return
$30,000 profit to each of the partners. And like an astute
Pyramid Investor, Cheryl spent only $5,000 of her take and used
the rest to buy out her partner. Within five months of the start of
her business career, Cheryl was the sole owner of a lucrative
company. What's more, she quit her job with the vet and set her
sights on a major expansion right away.

Believing she had to strike before competitors moved in to copy
her success, Cheryl started setting up Hound's Haven branches
in other rich and fashionable towns like Palm Beach, Palm
Springs and Beverly Hills. Obtaining extensive credit from a
local bank, she opened 16 new pet resorts in only the second
three months of her business career. When it was all over, her
company—now a corporation—was earning at the rate of $2.7
million per year.

Every Hound's Haven—except the Chicago branch—proved to
be a total success. Cheryl displayed an amazing knack for
smelling out a good business bet and for milking it to its fullest
potential. As a result, the former veterinary assistant was now
making $32,000 per month.

Success, for Cheryl, came stunningly fast. Her second investment
proved to be a Super Investment. There was no need to save for
future ventures. Her only responsibility was to manage Hound's
Haven to its fullest potential. She was free to spend all of her
earnings on herself—free to indulge. That's what she did—and
she deserved it.

She said good-bye to her two roommates in a cramped walk-up
apartment in Greenwich Village and moved into a Sutton Place
penthouse suite overlooking the East River. Nine rooms
decorated in the understated elegance of a regal Manhattan
residence. All hand-rubbed European furniture, French crystal,

Belgian tapestries and Italian art. It was her urban oasis—a showplace in the city.

On weekends, all thoughts turned to country living. Joined by her fiance, Geoffrey—a wealthy investment banker, she slipped behind the wheel of her yellow Jaguar convertible and tooled along the Long Island Expressway to the white and green mansion they rented on the beach at Southampton. From Friday to Sunday each and every week it was non-stop sun, surf and ice-cold Dom Perignon imported champagne. Casual living, like only the rich know how.

Cheryl learned quickly how to live to the hilt. She learned to demand the finest and to accept nothing less. When it came to designer clothes, haute cuisine and precision automobiles, her tastes and possessions matched those of royalty. And why not? Pyramid Investing had made her a wealthy woman. Her way of life simply reflected her lofty social and financial position.

For Jay B., the rise to the top of the business world was somewhat slower. Nevertheless, this young entrepreneur from College Park, Maryland applied the same proven principles of income balancing to pyramid $100 into a personal fortune valued at more than $10.7 million. And he did it all before his 25th birthday.

As a student at a Maryland university, Jay noted that most of his friends were perpetually broke, always scrounging around for a few dollars here and there. Since everyone was virtually penniless, bargain hunting was the biggest sport on campus. The favorite pastime was looking around for new places to buy cheap jeans, records and textbooks.

Jay never thought much of this until the Christmas vacation he spent working at a menswear manufacturing plant. He noticed that roughly 10 percent of the factory production was shipped to clearance outlets simply because of slight imperfections in the garments. Jay thought these so-called "seconds" would be a hit on the Maryland campus—a real bargain for the students and a good source of income for himself.

So he invested the $100 he'd made working at the plant and bought 25 leather-look jackets usually selling in retail shops at $27 each. He paid $4 apiece for the garments, resold them for $15, cleaned out the entire lot in two days and turned a quick profit of $275. He was on his way as a retail wheeler-dealer.

Making a long story short, Jay kept building on his early success. He expanded to women's clothes, junior sportswear, men's suits and even tennis gear. He bought entire truckloads of factory seconds, set up sales counters in the men's and women's dorms and moved his operation to other colleges in the Baltimore and Washington, D.C. area.

Jay's by-the-book approach to Pyramid Investing paid off. By continuously reinvesting a full 90 percent of initial profits, Jay was able to buy ever-larger inventories of "seconds" merchandise. This meant huge volume and big profits. Junior year earnings exceeded $8,000 a month and climbing.

At graduation Jay's personal worth exceeded $300,000, and he was ready to pull out all the stops. By living modestly through his college years, he'd put the principles of income balancing to practical use. He now had the means to set his master plan in motion—to set up a permanent retail chain selling "seconds" merchandise on every leading college campus in the nation.

Just like the first jacket sales in College Park, Jay's Bargain Boutiques Ltd. met with unqualified success in all of the fifty states. His "seconds" were the rage on campuses as distant and diverse as Pennsylvania and Texas. Everything from pre-shrunk denim suits to bulky-wool sweaters moved off the racks as fast as they were stocked. Like virtually every millionaire in history, Jay achieved fabulous wealth by filling a void. He found a way to reach college students with products they wanted and at prices they could afford. As a result, the money poured in.

Four years from the date of his first business venture—six weeks before his 25th birthday, Jay's personal accountants tallied his assets and informed the young man that he was valued at slightly less than $11 million. Only then did he shift the bulk of his annual income from business to personal expenses. He had arrived. It was time to indulge.

For Jay, that meant one thing. He purchased a magnificent 85-acre Tudor estate in southern Connecticut, played tennis daily, entertained beautiful women and supervised his business interests. He spent 81 percent of his income on personal luxuries and invested the balance in tax-free bonds and precious metals. The business itself remained his Super Investment—his ticket to permanent wealth, income, security and freedom. He was, as they say, "set for life."

Why did Jay, Cheryl, Lee and the other investors we've examined succeed while so many others fail? How did they manage, without fail, to turn shoestring investments into personal fortunes? How did they pyramid small business earnings into significant wealth?

The answer lies in the very basics of the Pyramid Investing system. Through use of the system, these now-wealthy people learned to spot the most lucrative opportunities. They learned how to balance income, how to parlay profits into successively larger ventures and how to build a fortune on borrowed funds.

Equally important, however, is that successful Pyramid Investors know exactly when to buy and sell their business interests. They've learned a secret you too can learn. That is: "How to trade your way to the top. How to buy small and sell big."

You'll have to learn this lesson if you want to earn the greatest possible profits. It's the only way to guarantee that you make the most of each and every business venture. Buying small and selling big lets you profit at both ends. You cut direct costs when you buy in, and you maximize the return when you sell out. There's no better way to pyramid earnings.

The first lesson in buying and selling is simple enough: Never buy into a business venture you believe is over-priced. The second lesson is just as clear: Never sell business interests below what you consider a respectable price. If you've developed a solid commercial enterprise, hold out until you get a tidy sum for it. That's the only way to parlay your wealth—to keep expanding your financial resources.

Remember, paying too much for a going business means you'll have to work twice as hard to produce a reasonable profit. A high percentage of incoming funds will be due your creditors, so there'll be less cash to put in the bank. That can delay your rise to the top of the pyramid by several years or more. After all, the sooner you amass substantial funds, the sooner you can make the Super Investments that will set you up for life.

Although there are literally hundreds of theories and guidelines for when to buy and sell business interests, none of the existing procedures are suitable for Pyramid Investors. You have special goals. You want to parlay small business earnings into astounding personal wealth. You want to go to the top—and you want to get there fast.

The following guide has been designed especially for you. It is recommended solely for the use by and benefit of Pyramid Investors. It lays bare one of the great secrets of successful investing: how to determine the precise time to buy and sell business interests.

Although you need not adhere to the guide down to the smallest percentage point, it is a good idea to include the basic data in your business strategy. As always, you are best off combining our recommendations with your own personal judgment. Every investment is unique, so you'll have to be the final judge of how to proceed in each case.

PURCHASING STRATEGY

Investment Stage	*Pricing Formula*
Investment one:	Stay below $500. You'll get started on the Pyramid system with little risk up front.
Investment two: $5,000 or more	Buy a venture earning at least ten times its selling price.
Investment three: $50,000 or more	Look for opportunities enabling you to quadruple your investment in 16 to 20 months.
Investment four: $1,000,000 or more	Seize the Super Investments—those likely to multiply your interests tenfold within five years.

SELLING STRATEGY

Investment Stage	Pricing Formula
Investment one	Hold out for 20 times the value of your initial stake. There's always a substantial reward for starting a successful venture.
Investment two:	Sell for nine times your initial stake. If your business is sound, you deserve a high premium for your hard work and lucrative ideas.
Investment three:	Look for a buyer at 11 times gross annual earnings, but be prepared to negotiate. Considering the high sums involved at this stage, it's unlikely you'll get exactly what you ask. Be willing to settle for 7.5 times earnings.
Investment four:	We recommend retaining Super Investment for life. If the venture is sound, it will serve as your passport to permanent wealth and security. You may, however, want to sell partial interest to achieve some liquidity. In these case, look for five times current value.

Work out your buy-and-sell calculations with the aid of an experienced accountant. You'll need a qualified professional to compute the data necessary for making management decisions. Like information on gross profits, pre-tax earnings and capital assets. Leave this to an expert.

Regardless of how successful you are as a Pyramid Investor, you may never feel at home with the ins and outs of accounting procedures. That's why even the biggest fortune-builders—like Paul S. of Cherry Hill, Pa.—usually leave the finer points of their business deals to highly paid staff accountants.

Paul has adhered to this policy from the day he started out in the business world. Even his first shoestring investment was observed and supervised by a well-known accountant. Although Paul couldn't pay his accountant much at first, he promised to keep raising the fees if the business grew. It did, in fact, grow in leaps and bounds, and both men prospered along the way.

Formerly employed as a draftsman for a Philadelphia-based architectural firm, Paul noticed the lack of good restaurants in the neighborhood surrounding the company's office tower. As a result, thousands of workers grumbled daily about the terrible food they were forced to eat, and many reluctantly brought their own lunch rather than pay high prices for tasteless meals.

As often happens in Pyramid Investing, what is viewed as a problem for most turns out to be a rare opportunity for the one person smart enough to see it. Paul was that one person.

Knowing a good bet when he saw one, Paul quit his job, withdrew $311 from the bank and started Feast-Ins International—a service offering moderately priced, quality lunches to Philadelphia's millions of office workers. The service offered wholesome, palatable lunches delivered right to the door.

For many, Feast-Ins proved to be the perfect solution to the lunchtime blahs. There was no battling the crowds, no fighting it out for tables, no more bouts with bad food and no tipping. Just about everyone seemed to like something about Feast-Ins.

That's why the business took off and just never stopped growing. Paul's $311 investment in food, menus and a leased delivery van was fully repaid in two weeks. What's more, within six weeks of operation, Feast-Ins was servicing 1,155 office workers and generating monthly profits of $4,000.

And that was only the beginning. A local business newspaper did a story on the service, and the media wheels started spinning. The radio and TV stations followed up with feature broadcasts, and a food critic topped it all off by giving Feast-Ins a three-star rating.

Publicity pushed the company's volume up to 4,132 lunches a day. Paul purchased an old warehouse and converted it into an automated kitchen, leased seven delivery vans, hired eight chefs and 36 deliverymen and started a promotional drive to sign up customers in every major office building in the city.

After five months as entrepreneur, Paul was well on his way to being a self-made millionaire. Feast-Ins was the hottest business in town—and still growing like wildfire. To Paul's way of thinking, this was the time to sell. For the first time in his life he wanted cash—a huge lump sum of it all at once. A stake big enough to buy his way into a really large corporate venture.

Working with an accountant, Paul valued Feast-Ins at $750,000. He put out feelers offering the business for sale at that amount and soon settled on a firm offer of $630,000. The selling price—a full 17 times current earnings—gave Paul the financial muscle to set up Feast-Outs, an international chain of fast-food eateries.

Six years later he was a partially retired centi-millionaire living in splendor in a palatial residence on California's southern coast.

"If I had to credit my success to a single factor," Paul says, "I would have to call it 'timing.' Selling Feast-Ins when it was a real hot property helped me get the highest possible price for the business. All that publicity the company was getting jacked up the value by about 50 percent. If I'd jumped the gun and sold too early, I think it would have meant a few hundred thousand dollars less in hard cash. That's important because you need every dollar you can get your hands on in order to pyramid your way to the next investment."

Timing. Leverage. Balance. Patience.

Time and again—in case after case—we've seen how these basic elements of Pyramid Investing can pay off for you. These are the secrets you'll want to reread, study, digest and then put to practical use in your own Pyramid strategy.

Like the pieces of a puzzle or the links of a chain, no single element of the Pyramid system can be ignored. The whole is only as good as the total sum of its parts. And in Pyramid Investing, every part is designed to combine to form a cohesive unit—a well-oiled money machine.

So study the system carefully. The more carefully you prepare, the better your chances of success.

ESTABLISHING
A PYRAMID TIMETABLE:
How to Grow
at Astonishing Speed

3

As a Pyramid Investor, you'll want to keep in mind one of the cardinal rules of our system: Never combine gambling and business. Like oil and water, they just don't mix.

Unlike other financial strategies, Pyramid Investing never relies on luck, chance, odds, magic or astrology. Ours is a calculated system—a detailed formula for achieving personal wealth. We never throw our chips in the pot and simply hope for the best. We initiate a series of tested procedures designed to achieve the kind of results we're shooting for. And we never settle for anything less than bull's-eyes.

Luck, of course, plays some part in everything we do in life. Successful marriages, businesses and careers all owe their success, in part, to luck. The beauty of Pyramid Investing, however, is that we limit the role of luck in amassing a personal fortune. We want maximum control over our ability to achieve the desired end—to become very rich.

Let's look at it in practical terms. The traveler driving from Maine to Montana would be lost without a map. If the driver relied on luck, he would probably wind up wasting much time and many miles—if, in fact, he ever arrived at his destination.

The driver with a good road map, on the other hand, could easily eliminate the wrong turns, the detours, the sense of going "nowhere fast." He could, instead, take the shortest route between two points and would likely arrive quickly and effortlessly.

The same is true with financial strategies. You need a map for this kind of journey as well. A map that will take you from the lowest rung of the economic ladder all the way to the very top. We give you this map. We call it the Pyramid System.

Everything stated in this book is stated for a specific purpose. All the charts, guidelines and formulas are your personal directions—your map to success. Follow the signs carefully; pay attention to every detail. The more carefully you prepare for your journey, the more likely you'll arrive on time and on course.

If luck be with you, fine, but don't wait for it to happen. We have a far better way to build a fortune than simply hoping for it. We'll show you how to go out and making things happen. How ordinary people just like you have amassed $10 million, $20 million, $30 million or more simply by launching a conscientious program of Pyramid Investing. The principle is sound—it can make you rich too. The sooner you forget about luck, odds and chance, the sooner you'll be started on the flight to success.

Keep in mind, as you proceed, that timing is crucial. You can't make wise business decisions unless you know how long it will take to build momentum, amass capital and gain operating experience. You'll need some indication of where you'll stand in a year or two down the road.

Your progress depends, in part, on your present financial status. If you're simply expanding a small business, the run to the roses may be quicker than if you're starting from scratch. Come up with a really good business idea, however, and you may make up for lost time and soar right to the top in a flash.

As we said, however, we like to leave as little to chance as possible. So we suggest you draw up your own personal timetable. A timetable designed to calculate how long it will take to earn your fortune.

Here's how it's done. On a sheet of notepaper, jot down one point for every statement which correctly applies to you:

- I have less than $250 cash on hand.
- I must borrow funds from outside sources.
- I must borrow from banks or finance companies.
- I have little or no business experience.
- I am starting my business from scratch.
- I am launching a manufacturing venture.
- I am working with a totally new and untested product or service.
- I must secure elaborate government approvals or licenses.
- I must hire workers from the very start.
- I must work with subcontractors.
- I have a poor credit rating.

You can figure out how long it may take you to make big money by adding your points and multiplying the sum by six. That's the approximate number of months' delay you'll face in achieving the various stages of Pyramid success.

For example, if you have less than $250 cash on hand, must borrow from banks and have no previous business experience, then you have three points against you. That means you'll face delays of about 18 months in reaching your business goals. So it may take 14 months instead of a year to make your first $50,000, 29 months instead of two years to make your first half million, and five years instead of four to reach the very top of the Pyramid—to amass enough cash to live the rest of your days in great wealth and security.

Obviously, this minor delay is a small price to pay to attain great wealth, power and prestige. But it is important to know just how long it will take to reach the various stages of the Pyramid system. Although your projections cannot be exact, they can help you plan for subsequent financing, staff requirements and business acquisitions.

Irv F. prepared a personal timetable to plan the expansion of his grocery business. Once a thriving three-unit chain, Irv's Food Shops had run into hard times. Declining volume coupled with higher operating costs took the steam out of profits and forced Irv to come up with new ideas.

The main problem seemed to be a change in the marketplace. All three shops were situated in similar neighborhoods near San Francisco's main business district. In recent years, the residents in the area changed from mostly older ethnic families to young singles and newlyweds. Failing to detect this transition, Irv continued selling the kinds of foods popular only to the older folks. As a result, competition moved in to service the young— and Irv's sales declined.

Irv's fortunes were on the rise, however, when he read an article about the Pyramid Investment system. Only then did he recognize his business problems as opportunities in disguise. Only then did he realize that this new and affluent market offered enormous profits to those ready and willing to accept change. For the first time he really believed he could make it big—big enough to join the ranks of the corporate giants. Big enough to own a nationwide chain of specialty food stores stretching from coast to coast.

His plan of action: to revitalize the existing shops, build up the profits and parlay the earnings into an ever-larger chain. To appeal to young moderns, he changed the names from Irv's to Le Pantry; remodeled from top to bottom using wicker, butcher block and lucite accessories; hired French-speaking sales clerks; and stocked the stores with popular items like frozen yogurt, crepes, imported cheeses and quiche pies.

The first stage was a clear success. Thanks to some creative advertising and timely publicity from the local newspaper, Le Pantry shops tripled the previous volume in only 60 days. Sales soared from $30,000 per month to $91,000, and profit quintupled to $21,000 in the same period.

Irv was well on his way. Like a good Pyramid Investor, however, he planned carefully for future growth. Most important, he wanted some idea of timing—how long would it take to go from a thriving three-store unit to 10 stores, then 50, then 250? The information would be important for lining up bank loans, buying real estate and signing construction contracts.

So Irv set about preparing his financial timetable. Using market research, accounting formulas and the Pyramid point system, he estimated it would take 8 months to acquire 10 stores, 15 months for 20 units, 26 months for 75 shops, and 4¼ years to build the full 250-store chain.

As it happened, advance planning proved invaluable. Whenever new markets opened up, Irv had the funds and facilities all primed and ready for immediate action. As a result, he was usually months or years ahead of the competition, and he built up a loyal following before the others even opened their doors.

"Taking the time to write your personal timetable is an effort that will pay off for you many times over," Irv notes. "In a competitive business like food retailing, even a month or two jump on the competition can make all the difference. So knowing in advance when I would be ready to open new stores really helped me get a head start.

"There's no arguing with success. My business grew into one of the largest mini-market operations in the nation. We lead in sales and profits in all the major cities—and we're still growing. The company grosses $45 million per year, and I own the whole outfit lock, stock and barrel. I'm filthy rich now—and I attribute a good part of my success to that first Pyramid Investment timetable. If there's one thing I've learned it's that in business good things go to those who are best prepared to take them."

Besides the business benefits, investment timetables can also help satisfy your personal needs. You'll probably want to know, for example, how long it will take to strike it rich as a Pyramid Investor. When you can design your dream house, buy a private jet or plan a trip around the world.

Your personal timetable can help provide the answers. It is designed especially for you. It is based on your specific needs, objectives and resources. So it can help gauge how long it may take you—and only you—to parlay small business earnings into the fortune of a lifetime.

You'll also use the timetable to plot your course throughout the Pyramid system. Like the navigator's compass, the timetable will keep you pointed in the right direction. You can only stray so far before the timetable tells you something's amiss.

Let's say, for example, you buy into your first $50,000 business venture with expectations of selling out nine months later at a tidy profit. If a year goes by and you still haven't made enough to move on, something may be wrong. You may not be doing enough to parlay your investment. Your management strategy may be off base; your products or services may be ill-suited for the marketplace; or you may be spending too little on advertising and promotion.

Whatever the specific problem, your timetable will probably help you track it down, because the timetable gets you re-examining your business strategy. If your timetable projects you'll be making million dollar investments in four years and you're still in the hundred-thousand-dollar class at that time, you know something may be slowing you down. So you start taking all the right steps to make up for lost time.

This delay in achieving timetable objectives is one of the telltale signs that a business should be sold. That's because as Pyramid Investors we believe in limiting risks. We believe a business in decline should be shored up and sold as soon as it can command a hefty price. There's no sense sticking it out with a venture that performs below expectations. We're interested in winners—the kind of winners that can make you rich ahead of schedule.

Getting rich quickly was Janet H.'s goal when she put her first Pyramid earnings—$61,000—into opening a children's nursery service in her home town of Wichita Falls, Texas. Since she'd earned every penny of this sum herself—parlaying a $75 investment in a tutoring service into a lucrative business—she wanted to make sure this next step up the Pyramid ladder would really pay off. It was her ticket to the top.

So she drew up a personal timetable based on the Pyramid point system. The calculations indicated a rapid rise to the top. Janet would sell her nursery service—Toddler Village—in nine months and would continue to parlay her earnings all the way to the million-dollar-plus category in little more than three years.

Nine months later, however, Toddler Village was operating profitably, but not profitably enough to command the $500,000 price tag Janet was shooting for. The major problem was attendance. Toddler Village's classes were only 70 percent enrolled, thus reducing the company's earning potential. Toddler Village simply didn't have the prestige appeal preferred by the area's wealthier families.

A very capable Pyramid Investor, Janet knew she had to act promptly and dramatically to boost attendance, improve earnings and sell the company. She knew she had to come up with an ingenious plan to make the company look better than ever so that it could command a premium price in the marketplace. Toddler Village was performing below timetable expectations. As such, it had to be sold quickly and profitably.

Janet's solution was nothing short of a brainstorm. Visiting a nearby university, she convinced the chairman of the child psychology department to serve as Toddler Village's headmaster. It was a stroke of genius. The professor was well-known throughout the southwest as an outstanding psychologist and educator. His appointment at the nursery convinced even the pickiest parents to send their young to Toddler Village. In just two months, attendance zoomed to near capacity and the company was producing record revenues.

What's more, the resulting publicity was phenomenal. Mention of the appointment in the *Houston Post* led to a full-scale feature article in a national woman's magazine. Toddler Village was touted as a leading example of the new type of children's nursery—one staffed by innovative professionals and geared towards psychological training.

Parents were not the only ones impressed by the school's accomplishments. Businessmen read the papers too, and many took an overnight interest in acquiring Toddler Village. For Janet, the scenario was just as she'd planned it. The former school teacher faced a seller's market. Competing buyers bid up the price of her Toddler Village. In the end, she sold out to a California-based conglomerate with interests in education and. leisure products. Her price: $607,000. Thanks to Janet's Pyramid timetable and her quick thinking, she pulled in enough cash to make millionaire status within arm's reach. As it happened, she struck real gold 15 months later by launching and running ADWEST—the hottest and fastest-growing advertising agency in the nation.

So what have we learned? Principally that the failure to achieve timetable objectives is a sign that a business must be sold. But what else do we look for? What are the other secrets of buying and selling small business ventures?

The following chart provides the answers. By pinpointing the crucial buy and sell signs, the chart tells you what to look for before you act. Each item listed is based on exhaustive research covering hundreds of business case histories. So study the chart and commit it to memory. It can help you sell your business interests at fabulous profits and can help you pick up new ventures for a steal.

SELL SIGNS

● Start thinking about selling out at the first indication of consumer resistance to your product or service. A new fad, trend, or superior item to the one you are selling may drastically reduce your market appeal in a matter of months. So act quickly. Don't wait for the roof to cave in.

● Uncle Sam can also mean big troubles these days. The first hint of expanded government regulation of your field or industry should be regarded as a sure "sell sign." New laws or bureaucratic controls may make it hard to generate the kind of landslide profits Pyramid Investors demand. So sell out before you are forced to spend half of your time wrestling with a legal octopus.

● Employee grievances can spread like wildfire. Gripes by one employee can lead to complaints by another, and another and so on. Before you know it, you can be faced with a serious morale problem affecting every aspect of your operation. Disgruntled employees, after all, are often angry, inefficient and discourteous. Since you'll never get anywhere with that kind of staff, it's a good idea to smooth over serious problems as soon as they arise and then sell out to the first high bidder.

● Believe it or not, a good dose of positive publicity can be taken as a clear sign to sell your business. That's because image can have as much to do with selling price as profitability. If your company looks good, it will attract a slew of buyers willing to pay top dollar. So strike while the iron is hot; sell out while the media spotlight is still focused on you.

● Watch for the signs of market clutter. As a Pyramid Investor, you want to find a void and clean up before the competition moves in. Having the field to yourself assures the kind of profits you need to parlay your assets into millions. Once you've made your killing, it makes good sense to sell out without delay. Changing your assets into cash before the stampede of competition arrives is the best way to snare the most money for your interests.

You can keep up on competitive activities by checking the real estate section of your local newspaper or business journal. See who's building or leasing new stores, factories or warehouses. That's the best way to keep tabs on potential competitors in your market area.

● Success, in itself, is another sell sign. Once your company has made its mark and is earning big dollars, that's the time to turn around and sell it. It will never fetch a higher price from prospective buyers.

As a Pyramid Investor, you must regard your business ventures as means to an end—as stepping stones to the top. Your only goal is to keep multiplying your cash base until you have enough to make the Super Investments that will set you up for life.

So be prepared to sell your businesses as soon as you can grab enough cash to ascend to the next level of the Pyramid. Whether it takes a month, six months or a year—waste no time in moving ahead to ever-larger business operations.

● Beware of fatigue or indifference on your own part. There comes a time when every entrepreneur wakes up and finds that some of the excitement of running his business has slipped away. The old charge just isn't there anymore.

In many cases, this feeling passes as quickly as it comes. The entrepreneur is back in there 101 percent in a matter of days. Once in awhile, however, personal indifference is due to a more serious problem—the owner-manager is really bored with the business and no longer cares about it.

If this happens to you, plan to sell out immediately. Indifference on your part will lead to inefficiency, poor employee morale and sloppy business practices. Before long, you'll be losing sales to the competition.

Since every business needs strong leadership from the top, your inability to provide this is a strong signal to sell. So if you find yourself in this position, put the company on the market, collect your profits and hunt around for a bigger and better challenge.

Remember the key lesson: Always sell from a position of strength. Let the "sell signals" serve as a warning to put your company back on sure footing before putting it up for bids. It's a good idea to look for buyers only after the "fires are out" and the firm is functioning smoothly.

We simply cannot stress it enough—when it comes to selling a business, image is as important as fact. The package that looks the best will command the highest price. What does that mean to you? Simple! Sell your business when it looks to the world like a flawless success. Like an unqualified winner.

BUY SIGNS

● Savvy wheeler-dealers the world over have learned how to buy wealthy companies at poorhouse prices simply by looking for "hidden assets." What does this mean? Simply that businesses are often put up for sale at prices far below their actual value. The reason: Owners do not recognize or understand the value of their property's hidden assets.

Here's where you come in. Let's say, for example, that a machinery distributor decides to sell out after three losing or marginally profitable years. Since the business is going nowhere, he agrees to sell for the value of the assets: $40,000.

The mistake here is in undervaluing the assets. In computing the selling price, the owner values the real estate at little more than the $11,000 he paid for it 40 years earlier. Since that time, the lot has become a prime retail location, worth approximately $200,000 to $230,000.

By purchasing this company—with its hidden and quite valuable asset—you would earn a minimum $160,000 profit from the day you take title. What's more, by developing the land for retail use you could probably resell it in no time at all and amass a healthy half million dollar profit to boot.

So when you hear of a business up for sale, take a close look before deciding how to act. Even if it's not what you've been looking for, hidden assets may make it too good to resist.

● Look for so-called turnaround situations—sluggish companies that can be returned to profitability simply by changing management. You'll find thousands of these ventures waiting for buyers wise enough to snatch them up.

It happens all the time. Poor management camouflages healthy companies, making them look worse than they really are. All the ingredients for success are there but are under-utilized. Management is simply too lazy, ignorant or indifferent to pull it all together.

Here's where you come in. By spotting a turnaround situation, you pick up a veritable money machine at liquidation prices. Remember, management thinks it's dumping a loser—but you know better. So you make a killing.

To spot turnaround situations, look for companies with a strong consumer franchise, popular products or services, minimal competition and solid growth prospects. These are the prerequisites for profitable operations. Add your promotional sense or administrative know-how, and chances are you'll have the venture squarely in the black in a matter of months. Best of all, you'll be able to Pyramid your initial investment ten or twenty times over when you're ready to sell.

● Changing market conditions can also make an unattractive company into a hands-down winner overnight. An influx of low-income immigrants, for example, into a transitional urban neighborhood may give new life to a bargain apparel shop. Thousands of new customers can easily turn marginal profits into a gold mine.

Your goal is to be aware of the transition before anyone else. You must sniff out the change before it is evident and buy into a local business while prices are still rock bottom.

How do you get advance information? How do you know when market conditions are likely to change? Simple: Be a first-class Pyramid Investor. Keep your ears open and your eyes wide. Judge everything you hear for its business implications. Pay close attention to news reports, government surveys and even the personal observations of friends and associates. You never know when you'll come across that tidbit of information that will make you rich. (One tip: To get an early report on changing neighborhoods, just walk in and talk to a real estate agent.)

● Just as good publicity can be a sure "sell sign," poor publicity may be your signal to buy. If that seems illogical, think again. Poor press notices can have a devastating effect on business, slashing sales volume by 30, 40, 50 percent or more. Frightened and discouraged, the owners may look to sell out as fast as possible.

This panic may spell opportunity for you. Why? Because the effects of negative publicity are often as short term as they are severe. Three months after a bad review, for example, a once-popular restaurant may be standing room only again. It takes extraordinary circumstances for bad press to permanently damage a successful business.

Fortunately for you, management may not be able to calmly wait out the storm. They may be begging for a buyer—and if you're ready and waiting you'll pick up a bargain. Use your judgment. If you think the bad reviews will blow over quickly, buy in and watch your investment multiply before your eyes.

Opportunity, then, is the key to effective buying. James R. of Miami, Florida knew this when he bought out all six units of the Happy Restaurant chain. Bad reviews in the *Miami Herald* had rocked the chain's business for several months, and the owners were desperate for a buyer. So James stepped in and made the deal of a lifetime, snapping up the entire corporation for $212,000.

James knew he was making a fabulous deal. Involved in Florida's restaurant industry for 21 years (as cook, waiter and manager), there was little he didn't know about the business. That's why his original investment of $409 in a pool snack bar had blossomed into a chain of concessions serving three major Miami hotels. By the time he had sold out, he'd already parlayed his earnings to more than $300,000.

Now he was ready for a really big deal—and Happy Restaurants proved the ideal opportunity. James knew that the bad reviews, blasting the restaurants' service, would have little effect on the great bulk of the chain's customers—tourists from New York and other northern states. Most would never even see the reviews!

Once the current crop of tourists left Florida and the new arrivals flooded in, the chain would again be catering to long lines of hungry vacationers. That's exactly what happened, and James's timing was perfect. He bought the chain and cleaned up the most severe service problems. Six weeks after he bought the chain, volume jumped by 40 percent and sales soared from $25,000 to $41,000 per month.

Then James went to work adding his own touches. He opened two new outlets near Disney World, offered breakfast specials and started advertising on local television. All three steps worked wonders. As a result, sales surpassed James's most optimistic expectations. Volume doubled to nearly $80,000 per month.

To top it all off, Happy Restaurants returned to favor with the press. Business editors across the state wrote prolifically about the chain's innovative practices and skyrocketing sales. Magazines, newspapers and business journals repeated the story many times over, making Happy Restaurants a household name to most Floridians.

Most important, the name became familiar to the State's rich and powerful investors. Soon the bids started rolling in—every businessman in the state, it seemed, wanted an interest in Happy Restaurants.

There was no doubt in James's mind—this was the time to sell. Just as he'd bought when the press was turned against Happy Restaurants, he'd sell while the company was basking in the glow of national attention.

The strategy worked. A giant Dallas-based food processor bid a whopping $2.7 million for Happy Restaurants. James accepted. He became a millionaire.

James's experience is not rare or unique. It is the natural outcome of a carefully controlled program of Pyramid Investing. It can happen to you.

As we have said, we leave very little to luck or chance. We plot our course every step of the way. As Pyramid Investors, we bring science to the art of business management.

Pay attention to our secrets for financial success, and you are likely to make millions. Take your time. Be patient and wait for the choice opportunities. And most important, select your investments with laser-like accuracy. Pinpoint your targets—and go after them with speed and single-minded determination.

If you want it bad enough, you can have your wildest dreams fulfilled. You can have your personal fortune. You can live like royalty. We'll show you how.

OVERCOMING THE 25 MOST COMMON MISTAKES:
Knowing What to Look for Will Help You Avoid the Traps

4

"It's not how much you make that counts, but how much you save."

That bit of advice is probably the single most important lesson for every budding entrepreneur out to make a personal fortune. For although you'll never find it written in the scholarly texts of leading business schools, it has served as a guiding principle for most of the world's great industrialists.

What does it mean? Simply that a lean, efficient and frugal business will succeed in the worst of times—when others all around are sinking into bankruptcy. It means that the business that saves money in its operations often survives, grows, prospers.

Like Henry Ford's early auto plant. The company wasn't always the industrial giant it is today. Back when it was still a young and shaky venture, Mr. Ford personally inspected every inch of the plant—every step of production. And when he noticed that a welding operation could be performed with two less drops of solder, he ordered it done. No questions asked.

You must be equally tough when it comes to guarding the purse strings of your own business ventures. If you minimize expenses in the early days—when sales are first starting to trickle in—you won't have to make as much to survive. And once you start making it big, the less bills you have to pay and the more profits you'll have on the bottom line. For Pyramid Investors that means one thing—a bigger bankroll for your next business venture.

This all leads up to a warning against the most common mistake people make when in business for themselves—overspending. All too often companies large and small regard the first indication of success as a sign to spend heavily. To commit large sums of money for elaborate offices, company cars, rapid expansion and expensive marketing schemes.

In nine cases out of ten, however, this overzealous approach backfires. Debt piles up, interest fees mount and cash flow deteriorates. The company has a hard time just keeping its ground—much less achieving significant growth. And bankruptcy—the ultimate demon—may be just around the corner. About 20 percent of all business failures, after all, stem from over-spending.

So avoid *Mistake Number One*. Examine every major and minor expense regardless of how essential it may seem at first glance. Approve of only those expenditures which support current operations, contribute to sales-producing activities and are more than likely to spur future growth. Put off everything that doesn't meet these criteria.

Mistake Number Two: Failure to Delegate.

Half of all business failures stem from owner-managers trying to balance 100 different responsibilities simultaneously.

Face it—you're only human. There's only so much you alone can do. Although as a small business person you'll naturally want to retain managing control over the company, there's nothing wrong with calling in expert help from time to time.

This is especially true in the areas you probably know little about. Like law, engineering and taxes. Trying to handle sophisticated work on your own can wind up costing you more than professional fees. Lack of knowledge about a simple tax regulation, for example, can cost you thousands in lost deductions.

Learn to delegate to employees as well. If you have people on the payroll, let them earn their salaries. Good workers want the chance to grow—to prove their worth and move ahead. Give them free rein to do so, and you'll benefit by having the best possible work force.

Remember, employees may notice things you are too busy to spot. They may have good ideas you've never thought of. Hear them out. Give them a chance to contribute. Some of the nation's largest corporations save millions of dollars a year thanks to ideas generated through worker suggestion programs. Start a program for your company. It makes good business sense.

To repeat, avoid the mistake of over-working yourself. Forget about trying to handle every minor detail on your own. Recognize when others are better suited to perform certain tasks.

Use the extra time to manage the major operations—to make the decisions that will affect your firm in the months and years to come. Delegate—it's a policy you'll profit from.

Mistake Number Three: Keeping Your Head in the Clouds.

One of the nation's leading business leaders—and one of the highest paid—has built a multi-billion dollar conglomerate by insisting on a simple corporate policy: "No surprises." This means that all managers are fully responsible for keeping the chief executive aware of business problems at their earliest stages of development. The feeling is that difficulties can best be handled before they have a chance to grow.

For small business people, this means developing an early-warning system designed to nip business problems in the bud. It means planning in advance for all types of negative developments, and it means establishing contingency procedures for handling even the worst projections. Knowing how you will act if the roof caves in is the best way to overcome the unforeseen problems of business ownership.

It all boils down to never letting success go to your head. Never get too busy counting the day's receipts to overlook the cracks just starting to show in the seams. Search out your business' problems. Listen for customer complaints. Take a hard look at production efficiences to cut out excess costs and material waste. And review long- and short-term cash requirements to make sure you always have enough money on hand to pay bills due. Keep one eye on today and one on the future. That's the best way to avoid the unpleasant "surprises" that can ruin you.

Mistake Number Four: Jumping the Gun.

Patience is a great virtue of the Pyramid Investor. Although you'll always be eager to move on to the next level of business ownership, it's best to wait until the cards are stacked in your favor. Most of all this means holding off until you have sufficient capital to start and sustain a new commercial venture.

All too many entrepreneurs jump the gun by getting started without the necessary capital. This is often a fatal mistake. Every new business needs enough reserve funds to cover all the unexpected expenses that crop up in the early stages. If the business is not as profitable as you think it will be, for example, there has to be enough cash in the bank to keep it floating until conditions improve.

Use this simple formula to determine if you are ready to move on to the next level of Pyramid Investing. Once you've spotted a new business you want to buy or start, total up the first year's sales and expenses on a monthly basis. Be very conservative. Figure the minimum sales and the maximum expenses.

If the projections indicate there will be early losses, add up the total deficit. This is the essential figure on which to base your plan of action. Make sure you have money to cover start-up costs plus twice the amount of expected losses. Don't get involved in the new business until you have this sum. It's better to wait and do things right than to act prematurely and fail.

Mistake Number Five: Projecting a Cloudy Image.

Just as a politician cannot fool all of his constituents all of the time, neither can a businessman please all of his customers. Too many companies go down the tubes trying to be everything to everybody.

The problem is one of image. In today's world, the accent is on specialization. The most successful companies are those that specialize in one or two things and do them better than anyone else. Like offering the lowest prices. Or the finest quality merchandise. Or the most dependable service.

Consumers must come to associate your business with one outstanding quality. When getting the lowest possible price on a television set is the objective, for example, they must think of your store as the cheapest outlet in town. Or when they need that prestige wedding gift for the boss's daughter, your jewelry store must be the one with the classiest immage. It is up to you to project the kind of strong, singular image consumers can identify and act on whenever they enter the marketplace.

This means adapting the modern marketing technique known as "positioning." You have to establish your business as one type of specialty firm, promote this image and stick with it. If you're a clothier, for example, let's say you identify your market as young men from 18 to 25. This means you'll have to stock high-fashion clothes, at moderate prices, in a modern and attractive shop. Diluting this appeal by carrying stuffy suits for older men as well will actually limit rather than expand your market. You'll lose that clear, consistent image consumers are most likely to act on.

So don't be greedy. Select your ideal market and exploit it thoroughly. There's plenty of money to be made serving a single type of consumer demand.

Mistake Number Six: Turning Your Back on Customers.

In the race to build an ever-larger business empire, entrepreneurs often forget that good customers are the cornerstone of every commercial success. You simply cannot go far without a solid base of loyal patrons.

Qualities that attract customers in the first place are often discarded, however, as the company grows in size and prosperity.

Suddenly, the owner-manager is too busy planning a new factory to have the time to service big accounts. The personal touch—so prevalent in small companies—disappears overnight, leaving customers feeling slighted and abused.

The main point is that customers want and appreciate small company services. So no matter how large your business interests become, always treat customers with that special courtesy they deserve. Stay in touch, personally, with the largest accounts, and allow only your best people to have direct customer contact. Go out of your way to fill emergency orders, to keep convenient hours, to offer liberal credit terms and to know Mrs. Smith by name.

Sam K. relied on top-notch customer services to build his Milwaukee-based mail order outfit from a one-man at-home operation to a $5 million concern employing 116 people. He did it by building a word-of-mouth reputation for reliability the competition couldn't touch.

Four times a year—every year—Sam sent a two page questionnaire to every customer on his mailing list. Do they have any gripes about Sam's services? Were all orders shipped on time? Did the products arrive in good condition? Did the merchandise perform in accordance with advertised specifications?

All negative answers were followed up immediately. Unhappy customers were offered substitute merchandise or a full cash refund. Letters were also sent extending the president's apologies. Customers appreciated the company's attention to detail and responded by reordering many times over the years.

At first, Sam handled all customer relations activities personally. Then, as the business grew, he hired well-trained assistants to handle the work. He retained a strong interest in the function, however, and continued to supervise it closely.

The larger a corporation grows, the harder it is to keep the small company spirit. But—as Sam discovered—it's well worth the effort.

Mistake Number Seven: Counting Your Chickens.

The best way to ruin a good business is to act on hope, rumor or chance. Basing management decisions on anything but hard facts can lead quickly to financial ruin.

The old warning about "counting your chickens before they hatch" never has more meaning than when it applies to business dealings. As an owner-manager you must know that simply wanting something to come true will not automatically make it so. You must be prepared to take the good with the bad—to suffer setbacks as well as victories.

If you have put in for a bank loan to build a new warehouse, for example, don't start construction until you get the OK from the mortgage officer. You may need the loan desperately, and you may feel you have an excellent chance of getting it. But you never really know until you get that call from the bank. And despite your rosy outlook, the answer may be "no." The world is not always fair or rational. You may very well deserve the loan but still not get it. It happens all the time.

Meanwhile, if you had started construction based on the hope of a loan approval, you might be forced to swallow heavy losses. Other banks may also turn thumbs down, meaning initial expenses for blueprints and land preparation would be lost forever. That's not the kind of drain you can absorb before soon feeling the pinch.

This precaution should apply to all your business dealings. If a supplier promises to ship new products at a special discount price, get the offer in writing. Don't lower your prices until you have the letter in hand. And when it comes time to order a hot new item, make sure you will sell out existing stocks before committing yourself to new purchases. The last thing you need is bloated inventories you can't unload at any price.

This kind of cautious thinking can save you thousands of dollars on unnecessary losses. Basing your decisions on hard, factual information is the best way to prevent costly mistakes.

Mistake Number Eight: Lack of Promotion.

Unlike large corporations, independent entrepreneurs often think they can run a business without promoting it. Somehow, promotions are perceived as wasteful, competing with the owner-manager's personal ability to build business. As a result, there is often little or no communication with the firm's existing and potential markets. No advertising, public relations or sales promotion.

This kind of thinking takes hold during the first months or years of operation. Since the company grows from its meager beginnings without the aid of paid promotions, management concludes that advertising is unnecessary. "We've grown from zero sales to more than $500,000 a year," the thinking goes, "and we've done it all without spending a dime on advertising. So why start now?"

The "why?" is very simple to answer—unlimited growth is not inevitable. That initial burst of sales to the half-million dollar mark may well be the firm's easiest success. As soon as moderate size is achieved, every extra dollar may have to be won at a competitor's expense. That means fighting it out for "market share"—and there's no tougher commercial battle.

Time and again advertising has been proven the best way to win a bigger piece of the pie. Huge and highly profitable corporations like Proctor & Gamble and Lever Bros. know that without advertising they would be reduced to a small fraction of their present size. Both are locked in fierce combat with aggressive competitors—and yet both are consistent winners primarily because they spend lavishly on effective advertising.

Well-planned communications can do wonders for small companies as well. No other vehicle, in fact, makes it possible for you to ride to the top of the business world in no time flat.

Take the now-famous case of a New York appliance dealer who used a simple, yet innovative advertising technique to turn a sleepy store into a $100-million-a-year empire. One of the first to use an informal approach directed at the city's blue collar workers, the dealer's advertising hit home with police, firemen, construction workers and the like. Hundreds of thousands flocked to his store, making the man rich a month after the first ads appeared. And in less than a year he presided over a vast retail and franchise organization selling everything from furniture to carpets to electric stoves. He was a multi-millionaire.

That's the power of advertising. It can work for you too. Use it!

Mistake Number Nine: Ignoring the Law.

Running a business in the 1970's is a more complex challenge than it was only ten years ago. The past decade has produced a dramatic rise in governmental regulations affecting even the smallest companies.

Independent entrepreneurs now have to keep up with a constantly changing arsenal of state, federal and local laws. Laws designed to protect employees, consumers and the public in general. Laws wide in scope and strictly enforced.

For the most part, these are new laws—the offspring of a nation increasingly concerned with business abuses. And they are tough laws, demanding close attention whether you run a small shop, a giant plant or a hugh conglomerate. Unfortunately, too many entrepreneurs believe that ignoring these laws will make them go away.

No such luck. There's simply no ignoring the likes of the Occupational Safety and Health Act (OSHA), the Consumer Product Safety Act (CPSA) or the Employee Retirement Income Security Act (ERISA). You must read the trade journals, speak with your attorney and stay up-to-date on all the provisions. It's the only way to survive in the modern business environment.

Why? Because failure to comply can wipe you out. Go astray of OSHA provisions, for example, and you can wind up facing a $10,000 fine and a jail sentence to boot. Worse yet, have a brush with the Consumer Product Safety Commission, and the resulting publicity may drive away the bulk of your customers overnight.

As you can see, compliance is not a choice—it's a must. So stay fully informed of all new and existing legislation. Keep an ear to the ground, listening for the latest rumblings from Washington and your state house.

Mistake Number 10: Extending Your Losses.

Wise gamblers and businessmen have at least one thing in common—both know when to cut their losses. They know that it is better to accept minimal losses and wipe the slate clean than it is to stick it out and run the risk of being wiped out.

What does this mean in practical terms? Let's take the case of Joe L., a young entrepreneur from Hartford, Connecticut. Joe used the Pyramid Investing technique to build up a very successful chain of home improvement centers. By age 29, he was already a millionaire.

That's not to say successful millionaires can't make mistakes too. When Joe opened his ninth home improvement center on a busy intersection in downtown Hartford, he was sure the store would be a winner. All signals pointed to a very healthy volume.

Unfortunately, the crystal ball was not working properly. Results at the store were disappointing from day one, and the hoped-for profits never materialized. Instead, losses started piling up, totaling more than $50,000 in the first six months. Still, Joe refused to admit defeat. This was his first setback, and he couldn't accept it. This stubbornness proved to be a costly mistake.

It took a year and a half for Joe to get smart—to close up and write off the Hartford outlet. By this time losses surpassed $100,000—most of which could have been saved by an early liquidation. It serves as a valuable lesson for all of us. A lesson that teaches us not to be "married," so to speak, to our business plans, ideas or actions. Not to forget that we are vulnerable human beings; we make errors. And when we do, we have to cut our losses and try again. There's no honor in the business world in going down with a sinking ship.

That's not to say you should drop everything at the first sign of failure. What looks devoid of all hope today may, of course, be tomorrow's greatest hope. But once you've given a business venture the old college try—once you've given it all you've got and there's no response—it's time to take out what you can get and move on to the next opportunity. There's no sense walking down a road when all the signs show nothing but red ink ahead.

Mistake Number Eleven: Too Many Cooks.

A group of friends who get along well playing cards or participating in other leisure activities will not necessarily make it as a business team. Although it often seems like fun to start a business with your buddies, such ventures are usually doomed to failure.

Why? Because the old saying about too many cooks spoiling the broth turns out to be very true. When a group of friends—or for that matter any group of equal partners—launches a company, chances are there will be too many leaders and too few workers. And without clear lines of authority and decision making, efficient operations are virtually impossible. The company suffers—and so too do the friendships.

The best advice is to start a firm with as few partners as possible. If you have all the cash to get rolling on your own, don't go out looking for someone else to take the fling with you. You're far better off assuming all the risks and responsibilities from the outset. That means you'll be in the best position to control the power and profits yourself.

A partnership is best only if two distinct talents can be brought together for a common goal. If you have money and your partner has the skill to develop new technology—that's a match. If you're an administrator and your partner's a salesman—that's a match. But if you are two friends just looking to work together, forget it. You are better off going it alone.

Mistake Number Twelve: A False Start.

Never forget that first impressions are the most important. In a business, that means making sure that things go right from the very first day of operations. Whether you own a store, factory or service outlet, the earliest days have a lasting impact on your future success.

Customers of all kinds are most critical of newly established businesses. They are actually looking for mistakes—anticipating them. That's why you'll want to do everything possible to run a smooth, errorless operation in those first few weeks and months of business. The impressions you make during this time will either help or haunt you for years to come.

So never open your doors to the public until you are absolutely ready. Overcome that initial eagerness by reminding yourself of the importance of making a good start. Jumping the gun will only help in turning off many potentially loyal customers.

Jack K. of Philadelphia, Pa., for example, never cuts the ribbon on his new variety stores until the entire staff is put through a full dress rehearsal of opening day. A day before each grand opening, a practice session is held. Mock sales are handled, typical complaints resolved and all likely problems discussed and reviewed.

The result: Jack actually receives complimentary letters from hundreds of customers pleased with the way the stores operate. That makes Jack happy—and rich. Why not try the same technique with your businesses?

Mistake Number Thirteen: Resting on Your Laurels.

The first taste of business success is a heady experience. It is so intoxicating, in fact, that you may want to give yourself a round of applause, lay back and savor your accomplishment. That's fine as long as this brief interlude does not give way to a state of lethargy.

For many entrepreneurs, the first success is so thrilling—so pleasant an experience—that they no longer want to risk failure. So they stop dead in their tracks, trying to live forever off that one successful store, product or idea. Although they may achieve this limited objective, they'll never make the kind of fortune Pyramid Investors have learned to expect.

All business history teaches us that as entrepreneurs we cannot stand still—we either move ahead or fall behind. Resting on our laurels is a waste of talent, initiative and momentum. If we've risked our money and talent and have been successful once, we must know that we can do it again. And we must try. It's the only way to parlay earnings into millions.

Within a year of setting up an export sales agency for small U.S. manufacturers, Connie U. had lined up 73 steady clients, hired a secretary and two assistants and moved into a plush office at New York's World Trade Center. She cleared $58,000 the first 12 months and was as happy as could be with her success.

But she knew that to keep her business strong she would have to offer better customer service. And that meant opening branch offices in five leading U.S. cities and two in Europe. The costs were staggering, and Connie feared failure. But she knew the kind of wealth and power she had always dreamed of would require more than a single success. She was committed to the Pyramid system.

And it worked beautifully. She branched out slowly, borrowing money from the banks and opening a new office every six months. Each proved immensely successful, and she soon presided over a worldwide corporation earning more than $2 million per year. The company went public seven years after its founding, and Connie was an instant millionaire. That extra push—after the first success—made it all possible.

Mistake Number Fourteen: Burying your Head in the Sand.

No one can argue that trust is a fine personal quality we all like to feel towards our fellow human beings. In the business world, however, trust takes on a different dimension. Extend it to the wrong people, and you'll wind up losing your shirt.

As a business owner or investor you simply cannot bury your head in the sand and say, "I have faith in people, and I'm going to trust everyone." Noble as that may be, it's also the best way to get taken for a sucker every time. And that's exactly what happens to all too many entrepreneurs who lose millions every year because they failed to keep close tabs on their business interests.

Unfortunately, many people are thoroughly dishonest when it comes to financial transactions. They will take advantage of every opportunity to steal and cheat. This is especially true of employees. Studies reveal that internal business thefts are on the rise and are a serious drain on companies of all sizes.

Statistics reveal that most frauds, thefts and schemes are committed by key company aides and associates. And here's the gist of the problem: After working with partners or hired managers for years, many owner-managers become lulled into a false sense of security. You start to trust those closest to you and never bother to check on their activities.

That can be a fatal oversight. Not only are long-term associates most likely to steal, but they can also do the most damage when they do. A top manager, after all, may have access to your books, checks and even cash reserves. One major scheme by a person on this level can leave you with little more than the shell of a once-healthy business.

Prevent illegal activities by extending your trust conservatively. Pay special attention to financial matters and have your accountant build in a system of bookkeeping checks to prevent employee fraud. Let everyone know that you take a hard line on criminal acts and that those caught will be fired and prosecuted. Sometimes just indicating that you are alert to fraud can do a lot to discourage criminal schemes.

Mistake Number Fifteen: Self-Fulfilled Prophecies.

Negative thinking is the greatest enemy of the business investor. No other mistake is as likely to result in failure as the willingness to admit defeat before you even start. Tell yourself you can't accomplish something, and you'll probably live up to this unfortunate prophecy.

It's a proven psychological phenomenon. Launch a venture you believe has little chance of succeeding, and you probably won't try as hard to make a go of it. Why should you? No one likes to invest much time, money or energy in wasted projects. So keep your thinking sound. Above all else, Pyramid Investing demands confidence. Confidence in yourself. Confidence that you too can build a personal fortune.

And you don't have to be born with this confidence. You can build it. Build it by refusing to give in to negative thinking. By telling yourself that you are as smart and as eager as the other winners who've made millions in our free enterprise system. By assuring yourself that you can do it too. That your dreams may, indeed, become reality.

Positive thinking alone won't make you rich. But it will help you to avoid that crushing self doubt so detrimental to business success. It will give you the will and confidence to make the most of the Pyramid techniques outlined in this book.

Believe in yourself. Trust in your abilities. You can do it. You can start with next to nothing and build a personal fortune. Tell yourself you'll accept nothing less.

Mistake Number Sixteen: Running in Every Direction.

For inexperienced entrepreneurs, the first taste of success is like the first glass of wine—it goes to the head. One profitable deal—one lucrative investment—and the individual feels invincible. No challenge is too great; no feat too difficult; no business unmanageable.

For those who get caught up in this superman complex, the results are predictable. The individual simply bites off more than he or she can chew. Rather than wisely concentrating on a single business venture, he or she makes a mad scramble to profit from a hundred different deals at once.

Problem is, it can't be done. Not in the Pyramid system. To make really big money, you must parlay your way to the top. You must cultivate each individual venture—one at a time—until it is ready to be sold for a handsome return.

Why do we stress this single-venture strategy? Because we believe that every business under your control deserves your complete and constant attention. It is, after all, your ticket to personal wealth. Treat it with care and respect. It will reward you in return.

Mistake Number Seventeen: Forgetting Your Business Umbrella.

Just like wise families, businesses must save for a rainy day. There's no telling when you'll want to call on your cash reserves to make up for unexpected losses or to take advantage of sudden opportunities.

The failure to put aside reserves can actually cripple your business overnight. Take the case of John R.'s Reliable Roofing

Company. John ignored the precautions of Pyramid Investing—and he paid the price.

Although he'd built up a respectable business servicing construction contractors in Trenton, N.J., John made a fatal mistake. By spending every penny of profits as fast as he made it, he left the company without a dollar of cash reserves.

By the time John realized the error of his ways, it was too late to do much about it. A long and bitter strike by local construction unions put a halt to all new housing in the area for nine months. That's nine months without a penny of income for Reliable Roofers.

Actually, the company didn't last even that long. After five losing months, the patience of the company's creditors was stretched to the breaking point. Landlords, suppliers and even the electric company were unwilling to extend further credit. John was out of business.

Cash reserves might have carried John through the tough times. Even partial payments would have satisfied creditors enough to keep the fires lit. But there was no money for anything; John himself had to look for work.

How much should you set aside for cash reserves? Depending on your type of business, we recommend 10 to 12 percent of your monthly profits. For risky ventures, such as clothing manufacturing, increase this to 15 percent. It's a precaution you'll be thankful for.

Mistake Number Eighteen: Under-Insuring.

Of all the tragic business mistakes, perhaps the most unfortunate is the failure to purchase sufficient insurance. It is most unfortunate simply because it is so easy to avoid.

Lack of adequate insurance can wipe you out before you know what hit you. And there's no telling when disaster will strike. Fires, floods, accidents—they rarely sound warnings. It's one, two, three and you're left without a factory, store or warehouse.

Problem is, too many small business owners look at insurance, of all things, as a way to cut corners. How foolish can you get! Operating without enough insurance is not economizing—it's gambling. And as Pyramid Investors, we don't gamble.

Sure, you don't want to be over-insured. And sure, your agent will try to sell you more than you need. We understand that. But still, there is a happy medium. Insurance is a crucial aspect of your total business operation. So take all the time you need to study your coverage requirements.

As a successful Pyramid Investor, you cannot risk parlaying your way to the $50,000, $500,000 or $5 million bracket and then blowing it all on a freak accident. You've got to cover yourself in every possible way—and that means buying more than just traditional fire, theft and liability policies.

Modern business insurance can protect you in the following additional ways:

- **Key Man Insurance:** Compensates the company in the event of the death of a top executive.

- **Business Interruption Insurance:** Provides for cash payments whenever you are forced to temporarily suspend operations due to fire or other damage.

- **Key Customer Insurance:** Keeps the cash flowing whenever a major customer is forced to close temporarily due to flooding, fire damage or similar circumstances.

Speak with your agent about all of the coverage plans available to you. Examine the alternatives and design a master policy that provides the kind of protection you need. When it comes to insurance, it's wise to abide by the old saying: "It's better to be safe than sorry."

Mistake Number Nineteen: The Wrong Side of the Street.

The three most important things about starting a retail business are location, location, *location!* Unless you settle on the ideal roost, you'll never generate the kind of volume you need to thrive and prosper in this competitive world. Even the hottest products, perched in the most attractive surroundings, can prove to be a total bomb unless you attract a constant flow of customer traffic.

Poor location may damage wholesale or manufacturing businesses as well. The reasons are numerous:

- Great distances between you and major customers may boost your distribution costs, thus reducing profitability.

- Too small an area may not accommodate future expansion. As a result, your company may be forced into a costly relocation.

- Launching an industrial venture on a retail site (where zoning allows it) can push operating expenses to exorbitant levels. Rents or mortgage payments may be as much as five or ten times the amount required for a more suitable spot.

So take this word of advice: Do a little market research before committing your company to a retail site. Stand by the location. See who walks by. Make sure it's the kind of traffic that will patronize your business.

Research industrial sites as well. Talk to commercial real estate agents. See what's available and compare the prices. Don't act until you find the choice spot. It could be the most crucial move you'll make.

As a final precaution, you may want to look over the available census reports. This will provide a clear picture of the market area, including population, age groups, income levels and competitive activities. That's the kind of data you need to make a wise decision.

Mistake Number Twenty: Knowing It All.

Like most entrepreneurs you're probably an independent sort. Strong, self-confident, assured of your actions. These are good qualities for Pyramid Investing. They'll help you go it alone— straight to the top.

There's a danger, however, in being too confident. That is, it can lead to stubbornness. And stubbornness has ruined more businesses than you'd care to count.

Having a know-it-all attitude is the closest thing to saying you're perfect—that you know everything. Trouble is, nothing can be further from the truth. As an independent entrepreneur, you need all the help and advice you can get from lawyers, accountants, advertising agencies and technical experts.

Granted, you may prove yourself to be very good at making money. You may have a way with people and ideas and may be able to parlay a $25 investment into $250,000 in two months. But the problem is, you are not out to make a quarter million dollars—you are out to make many millions. And until you reach the pinnacle, you ought to be open to good ideas whenever they come your way. It's the stubborn ones—the know it alls—who pass up even the best ideas. And they pay the price—a personal fortune remains an elusive dream.

Not that you have to accept every suggestion you hear. Of course not! But be wise enough to consider each and every tip before deciding how to act. After all, even someone you would never expect to have a good idea may come up with that one idea that's pure gold. It happens all the time.

When Goldie G. of Louisville, Kentucky started a lawn care service, she decided to handle the company's books on her own. A trained accountant, turned entrepreneur, she felt competent to do the work herself. The savings could total several thousand dollars a year.

Her company, Auto-Lawners, provided gardening services to homeowners throughout the Louisville area. In return for a regular monthly fee, Auto-Lawners did the mowing, trimming and seeding. The venture was Goldie's second step up the Pyramid ladder. She'd started out investing $130 in a small flower planting service.

Auto-Lawners proved very popular. Homeowners liked the company's economical rates and efficient service and were more than happy to turn over their lawn chores for the modest fee involved. As a result, word-of-mouth spread and the company soon boasted 35,000 customers. Goldie's investment was approaching a million dollar business.

Trouble is, more than 65 percent of the profits were required for reinvestment into new equipment. Mower-tractors, at $1,000 each, and trucks, at $9,500 each, were draining the company's coffers as soon as they were filled.

"I was talking about this problem to some friends at our country club," Goldie says, and Lawrence, an accountant, came up with a good idea. He suggested I lease new equipment, rather than buy. This would enable me to pay for new assets with operating revenues rather than with past profits.

"Although I was tempted to tell him to mind his own business, I had to admit to myself that his plan made sense. Just because I am an accountant didn't give me the right to play know it all. I would be the only one to lose from that kind of behavior.

"Anyway, Lawrence's idea proved to be the perfect tonic. As soon as I stopped draining profit with new purchases, the bottom line increased from $8,750 per month to $25,000 per month. That's more than $16,000 a month extra in my pocket. The lesson I learned: Keep an open mind."

Lesson learned.

Mistake Number Twenty-One: Inventory Ignorance.

Whether you are just starting out in business or are a veteran of 30 years, you may share a problem which is as common among the *Fortune* 500 as in neighborhood novelty shops. The problem is inventories, and the challenge is trying to strike a balance between supply and demand.

It is a delicate balance indeed. Carrying so-called "bloated inventories" can mean you have too much of your operating cash tied up in the warehouse or stockroom. The money could be put to better use as liquid funds, expansion capital or cash reserves.

What's more, excess inventory can lead to substantial losses. By stocking up on more of a single item than you really need, you may be stuck with many thousands of dollars of unsold merchandise. That's because styles or buying trends may suddenly change, and you'll be left holding the bag. That's the point; heavy inventories limit your flexibility.

Now you may think you have it all in perspective. The solution seems clear and simple: pare your inventories to the bone. Keep little or nothing in stock and buy only in response to customer orders. Sell off the warehouse, close up the back room and eliminate the risk of unwanted merchandise.

The only problem is that you'll be eliminating most of your business as well. That is because inadequate inventories are just as dangerous as excess goods. The failure to have the right merchandise ready and waiting for customers when and where they want it means lost business. There's no two ways about it. If you do not have what it takes to fill the order, competitors will. You can bet on it.

So inventory management is, as we've said, a balance. A balance between market demand, future projections and your own cash resources. You must ask yourself: How much merchandise will I need on hand today? How much tomorrow? Is it likely that sales will suddenly drop off? Will sales suddenly pick up? How much cash can I allot for inventories?

As a rule of thumb, we recommend that you keep the following percentage of your average monthly sales in inventory:

- Hot-Selling Items: 45 percent
- Steady Movers: 30 percent
- Moderate Sellers: 20 percent
- Slow-Selling Items: 10 percent

Try these guidelines and see how they work for you. Feel free to make the changes necessary for your particular business. As long as you are testing, experimenting and evaluating inventory decisions, you are moving in the right direction. The idea is to bring science to inventory management. To turn inventory ignorance into inventory intelligence. Do this, and you'll be way ahead of the crowd.

Mistake Number Twenty-Two: Ignoring the Basics.

As a Pyramid Investor on your way to a personal fortune, you probably have your head somewhere high in the clouds. You are eager, excited and itching with anticipation. The good life is just around the corner, and you can't wait to get there.

No doubt you have already learned that there is considerable glamour and dazzle in running your own show. You're an entrepreneur, an investor, a wheeler-dealer—and you're very good at it too. You're probably proud of your inventiveness, salesmanship and good old business sense. And you should be proud—you're getting rich.

The problem is, all this success and fanfare can turn your attention from the basics. And in business, numbers are the basics. No matter how good you are at drumming up sales, it won't amount to much unless you know where you stand on balance sheets, bank accounts, profit ratios and productivity.

Thousands of companies go down the tubes because managers disregard these basic business indicators. The feeling is that math should be left to the mathematicians; finances saved for accountants. The flaw in this thinking is that it is only half right. Although complex matters should be left to the experts, every business owner should be familiar with the basic concepts of commercial finance. It's the only way to keep tabs on your business where it really counts—at the roots.

What should you know? At the very least, you should be familiar with the following: balance sheets, profit and loss statements, sales to profit ratios, backlog, depreciation, accounts receivable, debt financing and asset-productivity ratios.

Knowledge of these statements and formulas can help you keep tabs on your businesses from the inside out. You'll know, for example, how much a new piece of equipment will probably return to you in extra profits. Or how much you'll have to boost sales in order to boost net income by 20, 30 or 40 percent. This data can be crucial when you are amassing cash for lucrative business opportunities.

You'll find all you need to know about the basics in a series of handy little guides published by the Small Business Administration. Just write to your local SBA office and ask for a checklist on small business financial publications. Most of the booklets are available to you free. Take the time to read them.

Mistake Number Twenty-Three: The Price Is Wrong.

Let's get down to brass tacks. As an independent entrepreneur, you bring products or services to market in return for specified fees. These fees are your compensation—your business income.

The question is, how do you determine if the fees you charge are adequate for the products or services rendered? How do you know you are being sufficiently reimbursed to earn a fair business profit? How do you know you are charging enough to cover costs, risks and personal expenses?

The answer to all of the above is "intelligent pricing." You must adopt a systematic approach to establishing prices—an approach that assures you of consistent profits after all costs and taxes are accounted and paid. Your goal, then, is to compute a balanced markup percentage—one high enough to be profitable yet sufficiently competitive to attract customers.

The determination of markup percentages can never be left to habit or instinct—to do so is a mistake. Yet many entrepreneurs set prices according to personal intuition; others rely instead on manufacturers' suggestions. Both are wrong. Pricing is too important to base on whims or generalizations.

Determining the ideal markup for your products and services is your responsibility. To do so, you'll want to consider a number of factors. First, the type of business you operate. Generally, markup varies from a low of 20 per cent in self-service food stores to a high of 50 percent in fashionable clothing shops. The difference is based primarily on risk. Clothiers must order fashions well in advance of the sales season, gambling that their selections will be accepted. Be sure to take a high markup if you are in an equally risky business.

You'll also want to consider the best way to achieve maximum profits. Pricing can have a major impact on this. Your choice is to seek a relatively high markup on a small sales volume, or you can boost the volume by reducing the markup.

Traditionally, large firms seek the big-volume, low-markup strategy while smaller outfits strive for high markup to compensate for low volume. Although a five to ten percent profit on sales may be satisfactory once you reach the big time, aim for a twenty-five percent return when you are first starting out. You'll need this kind of margin to parlay your way to the top.

If your small venture suddenly grows into a formidable enterprise, the time may come when you will want to reduce the markup in order to attract even more customers. When to take this step, and how far you can go, can be figured through a process called "equating velocities," which works according to the following formula.

Let's say your business is operating on a 33 percent gross margin and you are thinking of reducing this to 30 percent in order to draw customers from the competition. Before taking this step, you must determine the amount of increased sales volume you'll need to yield in dollars a gross margin at least as large as you now earn.

To get the answer, divide the present markup percentage by the lower figure under consideration: 33 percent divided by 30 equals 1.10. Thus, for every dollar of present volume, 1.10 or 10 percent more in sales will be needed to compensate for the lower markup. If you are relatively sure that the lower markup will boost sales considerably more than 10 percent, then the cut in markup is a sound business move. It will result in greater profits for you.

Now you know how to gauge your markup scientifically. Use the formula of "equating velocities" regularly. It's the best way to make sure your "prices are right."

Mistake Number Twenty-Four: Backing into a Corner.

Whether you understand the concept of "liquidity" or not, pay attention. It is a lesson you can never learn enough.

Put simply, liquidity is the ability to pay your bills. It is a prime objective of financial management. It answers the question, "Do I have enough cash, plus assets that can be readily turned into cash, to pay all of the debts that will come due this accounting period?"

The failure to keep your company sufficiently liquid means you cannot pay your bills. It is the best way to "back yourself into a corner"—to permanently damage your business.

You can avoid this mistake by testing your liquidity on a regular basis. Use the following formulas:

● Current Ratio is one of the best-known measures of financial strength. It is computed from the balance sheet by dividing current assets by current liabilities. For example, Javelin Manufacturing Company, with current assets of $140,000 and current liabilities of $60,000, has a current ratio of 2.3 to 1.

$$\frac{\text{current assets} = \$140,000}{\text{current liabilities} = \$\ 60,000} = 2.3 \text{ (or 2.3 to 1)}$$

This is considered a good current ratio. A ratio of two to one or better is deemed sufficient to keep the company solvent even in spite of minor setbacks. As Pyramid Investors, however, you should strive for an even greater margin of safety with a three-to-one or better ratio. Limiting risks, after all, is a key part of our strategy.

● Acid-Test Ratio is more exacting than the current ratio. By not including inventories, it focuses on the liquid assets. It is computed as follows:

$$\frac{\text{cash} + \text{Government securities} + \text{receivables}}{\text{current liabilities}}$$

For Javelin Manufacturing, which has no Government securities, this becomes $70,000 divided by $60,000, resulting in an acid-test ratio of 1.2 to 1.

An acid-test ratio of one to one is considered satisfactory, providing the company is in solid financial condition with little threat of receivables problems. Again, however, remember that as Pyramid Investors you should aim for the extra margin of a two-to-one acid-test ratio.

You can improve your company's liquidity by taking any one of the following steps:

- Pay off some debts
- Increase your current assets with loans or other borrowing
- Increase your current assets by adding equity, preferably cash, to the business
- Plow more of your profits back into the venture.
- Take any or all of these actions whenever your liquidity ratios fall below the suggested levels.

Mistake Number Twenty-Five: Hoping for the Best.

As Pyramid Investors, we cannot afford the luxury of hoping for the best—we have to demand it. At no time can you simply drift along dreaming of success without knowing how close you are to it.

Your goal, at all times, is to make a profit. If you are not making a profit, something is wrong. You must change—and change fast. You must get back on the road to Pyramid Success.

So instead of hoping for the best, you must learn to monitor your progress. A good way to do this is to develop a break-even chart. This mathematical device can help tell where you stand in dollars and cents. By indicating your break-even volume (the point at which you neither lose or make money), you'll know exactly how much you'll have to boost sales to generate substantial profits.

Break-even volume is the sum of your total fixed costs (costs which do not vary with the level of business activity) divided by the selling price minus the variable cost per unit of merchandise you sell. It looks like this:

$$\text{Break-even volume} = \frac{\text{total fixed costs}}{\text{selling price} - \text{variable cost per unit}}$$

In practical terms, let's say the Unnillel Corporation figures the costs for one of its products as follows: total fixed costs—$100,000; variable cost—$50 per unit. The selling price for the item is $100 per unit. This means that $50 per unit can be applied towards fixed costs. With fixed costs of $100,000; 2,000 units will have to be sold before any profit is earned. From that point on—after fixed costs are recovered—the $50 per unit sold will be profit.

The break-even point of 2,000 units is figured as such:

$$\text{Break-even volume} = \frac{\$100,000}{\$100 - \$50} = 2,000$$

A typical break-even chart illustrates the same data in more detailed form. The real benefit of the chart is that the distance between the two sloping lines shows the amount of profit and/or loss that can be expected at the sales volume represented by that point (note the shaded areas).

Prepare a break-even analysis for all your product and service lines. This way you won't be left hoping for profits—you'll know what to do to earn them. That's what Pyramid Investing is all about.

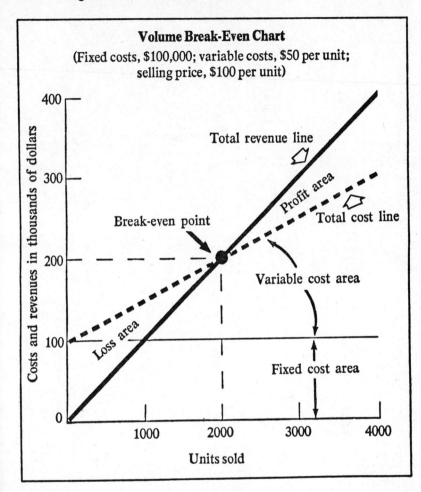

Volume Break-Even Chart
(Fixed costs, $100,000; variable costs, $50 per unit;
selling price, $100 per unit)

STARTING ON A SHOESTRING:
Proven Ideas for Starting
Out with Less Than $500

5

It's time to start making money. Time to launch your first business and get the dollars rolling in. You've had a look behind the scenes at the secrets of success—and now you're ready to put your lessons to practical use.

It seems like a long way to go. You have all the energy and ambition in the world but only a few hundred dollars to invest, and that's far removed from the millions you're after. Far removed, yes, but remember one thing—the Pyramid method is designed especially for you. For those who want to parlay a small nest egg into a personal fortune. That's the way the great millionaires—from Carnegie to Woolworth—have done it. You can too!

Step one is to do a little thinking. What kind of business venture will probably turn a nice profit for your small stake? Obviously, you'll have to avoid anything requiring a major capital investment. You simply don't have enough money yet, and the banks won't lend to you until you've proven your worth.

What's more, there's no sense in getting involved in an already competitive business. There's just no future in it. As the newest entry in a crowded field, you'll have to fight hardest for every dollar of business. Promotional expenses alone may wipe you out before you've had a chance to build a following—establish a name.

In this early stage of your career, it is essential to play the odds— to cut your risks to the bone. Don't look for a big killing now. That may come soon enough. Just look for the simplest, safest way to earn a respectable, moderate return on your investment. And look for something that will start generating profits right away. Any major obstacles to, or long waits for, profitability will simply eat up your small stake before it has started working for you. Your only goal at this time is to expand your capital base— to prepare for future investments in larger businesses.

The best bet is to work at home. This helps you get around the high cost of running a store or office and lets you put your money towards more productive ends. And as an added benefit, using part of your residence for business purposes may entitle you to a refund on personal taxes.

Also, do as much as you can on your own and with the aid of friends and family. Learn to rely as little as possible on outside services. If you need a letter typed, do it yourself—even if you have to hunt and peck. The extra effort can add up to substantial savings at a time when you need every penny you can muster.

And, most important, be original. Let your thoughts flow freely. Think back over your own experiences and ask yourself a simple question: What kind of new business idea have I always thought would succeed if it was only given a try?

Roslyn B. had the answer. After years of doing menial "women's jobs," she had recently latched on to an interesting assignment.

Hired by a major cosmetics firm to do basic market research, she interviewed other women, asking questions about the company's products. The job was interesting, and she was free to work according to her own schedule.

Best of all, the job gave her an idea. Why not go into business for herself? For the first time, it seemed possible. All she had to do was put her interviewing talents to work for local businessmen. Market research, she believed, could be as useful to small companies as to giant cosmetic firms.

As it happens, Roslyn B. hit on a winner—an excellent way to start a small company on a shoestring. Local stores, service outfits and virtually every kind of small business need to know how the public feels about their prices, policies and product lines. Knowing this, management can do its best to satisfy existing customers and to attract new patronage.

The beauty of it is that the service is rarely available to small, local companies at a price they can afford. Big, sophisticated research firms are out of their budgets, and enterprising entrepreneurs have not stepped in to offer an economical alternative.

Until now! This could be just the opportunity you've been waiting for. Regardless of where you live—no matter how small the community—chances are good that business people are just waiting for the service you can offer.

Here's how it works:

Comb the yellow pages for the names of all consumer-oriented companies like dress shops, food stores, service stations and movie theaters in your area. Divide the names into two lists: larger units, such as supermarkets and department stores, and smaller outlets, such as grocery stores and beauty salons.

Next, prepare a sample questionnaire indicating the kinds of questions you would ask consumers about these businesses.

- Where do local residents shop for food?

- Where do they buy paint and hardware?

- If a woman is a regular at Carla's Beauty Salon, what inducement would make her try Marie's? Lower prices? Better service?

- What new services would shoppers like to see local stores provide? Free deliveries? Credit plans?

- What's the best run shop in town? Why?

Think out your questions carefully. Include everything you think local business people would like to know about themselves and their competitors.

Now you're ready to make your first contacts. Visit all prospects in person, starting with the larger firms on your list. Winning over a big customer or two right away may convince the smaller ones to follow suit.

Speak only to company owners or managers. Explain that you've started a new market research service in town and that you'll be providing business customers with valuable consumer information. Information they can use to keep customers happy and to attract new sales, such as what people want, demand and expect from local shops. And what owners can do to lure business away from competitors.

Show your questionnaire and offer to let prospective customers add three questions of their own to the list. This personalized touch may convince many to sign up for your service—there's simply no other way to get such useful consumer information.

Be sure, however, to work out a realistic price policy. Small companies will not spend a lot of money on non-essential services no matter how worthy they may be. So keep your fees down to $25 per month for the smallest outfits, $35 for the middle range and a top of $50 for the larger units. You'll have to make your money by signing up a sizable roster of clients rather than by trying to soak a small number of firms with hefty fees.

Roslyn B.'s sales campaign took off like a jet from the very first week. After she signed up the largest discount store in her home town of Yonkers, N.Y., the rest came easy. She convinced the local newspaper to do a short feature on her service, and the resulting publicity brought the customers to her. In addition, she used the clipping as a promotional piece and found it to be of exceptional help on future sales calls.

This two-pronged program of aggressive selling and clever promotions did the trick. Within three months Roslyn's service boasted 140 subscribers bringing in monthly fees of $4,900—an annual income of $58,800. All of this on an initial investment of only $276 for stationery, gasoline and telephone calls.

In the first 12 months, Roslyn cleared a profit, after subtracting all interviewing expenses, of $20,011—more than enough to leave the first stage of the Pyramid and to invest in a much larger business venture. What's more, she sold off the market research service to a neighbor—a retired plumber—for $35,000 cash. She was on her way!

Clyde J., a bank clerk with aspirations of starting a business of his own, needed something he could work on in his spare time. Something requiring a small capital investment but offering unlimited opportunities for rapid growth. All he had to invest was the $311 he'd managed to save from his paychecks—and he wanted to parlay this amount quickly so he could build the restaurant he'd been planning for years.

But first things first. He hit upon a great idea for his starting venture. Knowing that his East Los Angeles neighbors were forever complaining about the lack of available craftsmen in the area, Clyde decided to make life easier for others while making a profit for himself. He set up the community's first Service Referral Center, making available to local residents the names of competent plumbers, electricians, house painters, paper hangers, gardeners, and the like. All of the craftsmen listed with Clyde's service were independent contractors working for less than the exorbitant rates charged by high-powered professionals. That was just the kind of price-break inflation-weary consumers were looking for—and they embraced Clyde's service overnight.

Clyde chalked up hefty profits at both ends. The contractors paid him an annual fee of $100 each to be listed with the service, and consumers paid $3 apiece for every referral. It worked like this:

Let's say Joe R. is a Los Angeles cop who does carpentry in his spare time to earn some extra income. By listing with Clyde's service, he's likely to get all the business he can handle without advertising on his own or knocking on doors soliciting jobs. The $100 fee will probably be covered in the first week or two of work.

In the same vein, local homeowners know that by turning to Clyde they'll get the names of carpenters, like Joe, who work below the going rates. They simply drop Clyde a note, along with a $3 check, asking for the names of reputable craftsmen in their areas. Clyde checks his listings, jots down three names and forwards a response in the return mail. Considering that homeowners may save from $50 to several hundred dollars on a single job this way, the $3 fee is a worthy investment.

Clyde, too, learned the beauty of low-cost promotions. Rather than investing in expensive advertising, he prepared small publicity cards for display on church and community bulletin boards. In addition, he asked his contractors to talk up the service to friends, neighbors and fellow workers.

As with every good, legitimate service consumers really need, word-of-mouth spread quickly. In less than four months, 226 contractors were registered with Clyde's service, and referrals were pouring in at the rate of 80 per week. So a part-time business, run at night from his apartment kitchen, was netting Clyde more than $35,000 a year in extra income.

It was more than he had ever imagined in his wildest dreams. And in little more than a year he took the ultimate step. Armed with a $28,000 cash down payment, he got the OK on a loan for his first restaurant. Clyde J. was now a businessman.

Selling intangibles is not the only way to make it big on a small investment. Believe it or not, you can start right in selling consumer products even if you have less than $500 to spare.

The secret is to select low-cost, high-margin products and to aim for small, specialty markets. It is also a good idea to pick something the major manufacturers are not yet selling. Getting in on a new trend or fad just as it's taking off is the best way to make a killing before the big competitors move in.

Do just what the experts do. Select a limited sales territory and "position" yourself as the only local supplier of the product you're handling. Let customers test your product for sales appeal, try to make any changes in the product they think will help it, and offer very liberal payment terms to start. Once the product gains momentum and develops a following of its own, then you can expand your base of operations and can demand better terms from retailers.

Betty Z. had the right idea. By subscribing to the leading high-fashion magazines like *Vogue* and *Glamour,* she was able to spot the new fashion trends at the first sign of popularity. So when she noticed that hand-lettered T-shirts were becoming the rage with the jet set on the French Riviera, she knew it wouldn't be long before men and women in her home town of Princeton, New Jersey would be clamoring for one in every color.

And she was determined to profit from it. So she started making hand-lettered T-shirts in her basement—and she found it simple and easy to do.

First, Betty visited a large T-shirt manufacturer near the state capital in Trenton. She made a deal to purchase an initial order of 200 plain-white T-shirts for 85 cents each—just slightly above wholesale. Then she laid out another $35 for dyes and stencils and went to work making the first 50 shirts. In two weeks, she was ready to start selling.

Mapping out a list of the chic shops in and around Princeton, she started visiting with the proprietors one at a time. And she went armed with a *Vogue* magazine clipping showing tanned jet-setters sporting initialed T-shirts on the beaches of Cannes. If her talk didn't convince the merchants that a trend was in the making, her clipping did.

Betty worked out a trial arrangement with all interested parties. They could keep ten T-shirts on consignment, paying her only if the merchandise was sold. This encouraged retailers to try the samples. They had nothing to lose if the product flopped. If the merchandise moved, Betty received $6 per shirt—a 600 percent profit over the total costs of goods, dyes, stencils and transportation.

Getting the product on display proved more difficult than it had seemed. Only two of the first six stores Betty visited agreed to handle the shirts. Betty was frustrated, but she hung in—and her patience paid off in no time.

As soon as some of the more fashionable people started appearing around town in Betty's shirts, the rage was in full bloom. Everyone wanted initialed shirts, and Betty had the only show in town. She was soon selling from 36 shops throughout southern New Jersey and was doing an equally good volume through mail order requests.

Betty hired three college students on a part-time basis to handle the workload, set up a corporation called U-shirts, and was soon selling more than 800 shirts a week to customers around the country. She liked the business, remained with it for two years and drew down an annual salary plus profits of more than $31,000.

Although the craze is still going strong—and has branched out to initialed hats, umbrellas and bags—Betty had made enough to sell off and embark on her dream of dreams: to open a high-fashion boutique of her own in Palm Beach, California. That's exactly what she did, and she made an instant success of it too! How? Simply by using the same magazine trend-spotting approach she'd used to make her first killing in the business world.

Now you see how it's done. How a small investment can put you on the road to a personal fortune. How hard-working people just like you have parlayed a good idea and a few hundred dollars into a pile of money.

Want some other small-investment strategies? See if you can make a bundle on these proven winners:

- Open a by-appointment boutique right in your home. Sell anything from antiques to modern art. Start with a small inventory, word-of-mouth promotion and a smattering of local advertising. Many people like the personal touch of one-to-one shopping. Do things right, and you'll win their business.

- Turn your craft or hobby into profits. Sell ceramics, paintings, sculpture and the like in your home, through retail shops and at flea markets. Also, enter exhibitions and contests whenever possible. Who knows, you may very well make a name for yourself and start pulling down big prices for your work.

- Launch your own Party Planning Service. Specialize in planning and coordinating private affairs from weddings to anniversaries. Offer to select the cards, book the room, hire the band and choose the flowers. Base your fee on the amount of work involved and the size of the affair ($2,000 is reasonable for a big wedding). Make things run smoothly, and you'll probably build a following in no time at all. More and more people are now seeking professional help when planning that once-in-a-lifetime occasion.

  Get started by investing in high-quality printed cards announcing your new service. Send them around to all churches, synagogues, caterers and community organizations. Get that one chance to prove your worth, and you may be well on your way.

- Get in on the new mini-mall movement that's spreading across the country. The malls are actually permanent, indoor flea markets where hundreds of small vendors come together to sell a variety of goods.

The benefits to you are exceptional. You get your own sales stall for a fraction of the cost of a retail store. All you pay is a small monthly fee, and there are no hidden costs for maintenance, insurance or heat. What's more, millions of consumers are turning to this type of shopping in search of bargains, variety and just for the fun of it. So the sales potential is unlimited. Watch the business opportunities section of your newspaper or the *Wall Street Journal* for news of a mall opening in your area.

Our free enterprise system is rich in opportunities for any individual—man or woman, young or old—willing to devote a little time, energy and creativity to making a personal fortune. The old saying that "money goes to money" is just an excuse for the lazy. Any list of the super-rich includes the names of many who never had a dime until they took the first step on the road to wealth.

Join them! The sooner you start, the sooner you'll get there. Use any of the case histories mentioned in this chapter or come up with an idea of your own. Almost any unique and original idea is enough to get you off the ground. Once you get rolling, there's no telling how far you'll go. We'll show you how to multiply everything you make into an ever-larger fortune.

THE BASE OF THE PYRAMID:
Money-Making Investments
for Your First $5,000

6

Sanford K. started a telephone referral service in his home town of Denver, Colorado. He knew exactly what to do with the first $5,000 in profits he cleared. He turned right around and poured the money back into a new investment.

And not just any investment at that. To earn the kind of personal fortune Sanford had his eye on, he knew he would have to follow the principles of Pyramid Investing carefully. And in the early stages, that means spotting highly profitable business opportunities requiring modest amounts of initial cash. The secret is to find a void and fill it. Like billionaires from Ford to Onassis, Sanford knew he would have to come up with a product or service customers would be clamoring for.

He found just the thing. Knowing that some of the world's giant corporations started out selling by mail, Sanford looked into the idea and liked what he found. By investing a few thousand dollars in a mail order operation, average men and women have parlayed small nest eggs into multi-million dollar concerns.

Typical of this success is a mail order house in New York that Sanford spent a few days observing before launching his own. Started by the owner of a one-man shoe store as the way to make a few extra bucks on the side, the venture has grown into a $5 million per year business employing more than 100 people in showrooms, warehouses and order facilities across the state. The founder is now a millionaire several times over—all on a tiny investment to cover initial postage costs and advertising.

Sanford was wise enough to know he'd have to come up with a unique approach to make mail order work. Something not generally available through retail stores or other mail order outfits. And he hit on just the brainstorm he needed while reading through some well-known business publications.

Many American women, it seems, have a hard time finding small- and petite-size clothes in stylish fashions at local retail shops. Merchants simply refuse to carry sizes one, three and five on the belief that the market for such items is too small to cater to.

Sanford recognized this immediately as a great opportunity. Although stocking tiny sizes may not be profitable for stores, it is just the thing for a mail order business. Mail order merchants can tap a far larger market, reaching consumers across the nation. Every small-sized woman from Maine to Alaska is a potential customer—and an eager one at that. For the first time, someone would be specializing in exactly what these women have been searching for—fashionable petite clothes in a wide assortment of colors and styles.

Also, mail order ventures can operate at a much lower cost than high-overhead retail units. Goods need not be ordered in bulk until they are proven sales winners. This cuts the risk of heavy losses or excessive inventories and makes it possible to sell in a big way without laying out a lot of cash up front.

Selling by mail order also lets you work right in your home. Since there is no need for expensive display areas, you can do without high-rental leases, store maintenance and insurance. All the savings come right back to you as extra profits.

Coming up with an effective list is the key to mail order success. One way to do this is to buy or rent a list from the numerous outfits specializing in this service. You simply indicate the kind of market you want to reach, and they'll provide a list designed to produce a substantial response.

If the right list is not available, you are better off designing your own. Take out an advertisement or two in newspapers or magazines likely to be read by your target audience. Describe your service, offer your most appealing product and include a clip-out order form in the ad. The names of the people responding will form the foundation of your list. More ads, additional orders and word-of-mouth will combine to expand your list and your sales.

It certainly worked for Sanford. A single ad in a popular woman's magazine yielded 1,211 orders for an imported French bikini selling for $32. That's more than $38,000 in sales resulting from a single ad costing less than $1,000. And success like this is no freak accident. It happens virtually every time you are the first to find and offer a service consumers want.

Once you find a good bet, stick with it and milk it for all it's worth. Corner the market. Get a jump on potential competitors. Expand your appeal and improve your services. Experiment with new ideas until you know the best way to yield the biggest return.

But whatever you do, don't make the same mistakes that lead many young, explosive companies down the road to failure. Most of all, don't let your new-found wealth slow your business energies. Never sit back and rest on your laurels. You're on the

ladder to great success now, and you have to keep moving to get
to the top.

Take the case of Marion R. Her first ad for women's needlepoint
tennis racket covers produced 611 orders at $21 each—a total of
$12,831. Since she made the covers herself, there was no way she
could complete the order single-handedly in time to satisfy
customers.

What did she do? Well she certainly didn't turn her back on
what proved to be a business gold mine. Rather than settling for
a share of the orders she could complete in time, Marion went
right out and hired assistants to complete the entire production.

And she didn't stop there. While working on the first order, she
placed two more ads in the original publication and tested the
response in three new magazines. The orders kept rolling in, and
she knew she was on to a sure thing—a winner that would make
Marion R. a rich woman.

To improve her operation and to keep the money flowing,
Marion continuously tested new publications for her mail order
ads. Those that produced were scheduled for more and larger
ads—those that didn't were scratched from the list and replaced
by others. In time, she knew exactly where to get the best
response for the lowest cost—and results proved it. Orders were
pouring in at the rate of between $50,000 to $65,000 per month.

To compound a good thing—and to trade on the reputable name
she'd established—Marion expanded her line, opening whole
new profit opportunities. First came needlepoint tennis
equipment pouches, then golf caps and finally a full line of
Marion R. signature sports blouses.

Quite to her surprise, Marion R. designs became "the thing" on
many fashionable suburban golf courses and tennis courts. Her

products were featured in most of the leading women's magazines as well as in pro shops and exclusive boutiques across the nation. Marion R. had graduated quickly from the small business class—she was now a major entrepreneur on her way to a personal fortune.

Everyone can use and adapt similar techniques for personal success. When you strike the market with a hot product or service, promote it hard. Pour back at least 70 percent of all initial profits into the business. Advertise, offer new lines and hire a staff if need be. This is the best time to build a solid base for future growth.

Another point: Be a tough negotiator. Everyone loves a winner, and everyone will want to share in your wealth and success. So when wholesalers, distributors and the like come around to make deals, be sure to drive a hard bargain.

Marion R., for example, asked three concessions from all retailers interested in carrying her line: long-term commitments, heavy advance orders and prime display areas. She won them all—and you can too if you strike a good idea and manage it well.

Sometimes, all you have to do is look like a success, and the world will make you one. That's part of the trick to getting started in the phenomenally lucrative field of "Odd Lot Trading." With little more than a telephone and an office, you can be wheeling and dealing with the *Fortune* 500—making deals for more money than you thought you'd earn in a lifetime.

In this little-known business, image is the key to the mint—the secret to getting your foot in the door. So that's where your initial investment must go—to projecting the image of an already established and successful corporation. You have to look the part to deal with the nation's leading companies. They simply won't do business with inexperienced upstarts.

Take the case of Harry B.—a savvy entrepreneur in business for himself ever since his first high school paper route 20 years earlier. His numerous ventures—from retail shops to distributorships—always earned a respectable living, but he'd never made the killing he always dreamed about. Now, with odd lot trading, the big money seemed within reach!

Taking the $7,200 he'd recently made selling men's shirts on consignment, Harry invested carefully to project a prosperous image. First, he dreamed up the name Global Ventures Limited and incorporated under it. Then he went out and rented a plush office, hired a top-notch secretary, ordered fine embossed stationery and bought the most expensive silk-finish business cards money could buy. To top it all off, he plunked down $500 on a custom-tailored suit that literally reeked of wealth.

Then he set off creating the cornerstone of odd lot trading— establishing good contacts. The business itself is simple enough. Here's how it works:

From time to time, the nation's manufacturers produce more than they can sell. More radios, televisions, carpets or calculators than the market will absorb. Even the biggest names in American industry make this mistake, projecting demand to be far greater than it actually is.

As a result, inventories pile up, forcing the makers to seek alternate distribution. In most cases, prices are slashed and the goods are dumped in foreign markets or are sold to discounters. An electronic calculator moved this way may bring $9, compared to the standard wholesale price of $21. Still, the manufacturers are happy for whatever they can get.

And that's where odd lot traders come in. By developing good contacts on both sides of the fence—manufacturing as well as selling—they get the first call when big producers have to unload excess merchandise. Prove you can produce, and you'll be entrusted with hundred-thousand dollar deals on a regular basis. And the beauty of it is, you don't have to put up a penny of your own money until a buyer is found.

It started paying off for Harry almost overnight. For one month he made the rounds, introducing himself to exporters, discounters and manufacturers around the nation. Everyone big enough to buy or sell bulk merchandise was on his list. All visits were followed up with a personalized letter designed to build recognition for the Global Ventures name.

The second day back in his office lightning struck.

The caller: A large ladies' apparel manufacturer in Delaware.

The problem: Could Harry find a buyer for 35,000 velvet dresses at $14 each (originally $26 wholesale).

The solution: Three calls later Harry tracked down a Dallas-based outlet chain eager to accept the order at $13.50 per dress, with the labels removed.

The profit: In only a few minutes Harry earned a $52,500 commission. There was no risk, no capital investments, no headaches. Once a verbal agreement was set, lawyers handled all the paperwork. The goods were shipped directly from Delaware to Dallas, and Harry picked up his profit without delay.

What's more, he'd closed his first big deal, established a track record and made a name for himself. That's the kind of experience a trader needs to keep the phones ringing—to keep the business coming. Although success may not always come as fast as it did for Harry, once you get started you'll find the opportunities to make big money are virtually unlimited.

Keep in mind, however, that odd lot trading demands discretion. Corporate sellers never want it known that they have goofed on production runs or that they are dumping top-quality goods at distress prices. That kind of news makes for bad public relations.

So keep your deals secret. Shy away from publicity. Let word-of-mouth among the companies themselves build your reputation. It's the best way to grow in this unique and highly profitable business.

BUILDING ON SUCCESS:
How Four Entrepreneurs
Turned $50,000 into Millions

7

A wise man once said that "nothing succeeds like success." Truer words were never spoken. Once the ball is in your court—once you've started making big money—the advantage is in your favor. You have power, control and influence—and you can use it to triple, quadruple or multiply your wealth ten times over.

Most important, when things start going your way, you have momentum. And that's the ideal time to reinvest and expand your fortune. The sophisticated system of Pyramid Investing, in fact, is built on a simple premise—that you must strike when the iron is hot.

By the time you're ready for the really big investments of $50,000 or more, you'll probably be awed by the great sum you've already made. Just the fact that you have $50,000 to invest when you started with less than $500 is likely to make you just a bit lightheaded. You may even be tempted to stash away what you have made, lock it up and leave the business world with a sizable treasure.

Don't do it! If you are really serious about making big money, now is the time to put your chips back on the table. The odds are in your favor. According to figures compiled by the Economics Division of Dun & Bradstreet, roughly 80 percent of business failures are due to financial problems, such as inadequate capital. For the most part these problems are behind you now—your chances for continued success are vastly improved.

What's more, once you are firmly established the likelihood of business failure decreases every year you stay in business. The failure rate for the second year of operation, for example, is about 14 percent; for the sixth year it drops to 7 percent. And it keeps going down. By the time you've been in business for ten years, the chance of going bankrupt drops to 2 percent.

Of primary importance is the fact that you now have enough money to invest in a really large business. The business that can make you a millionaire. That can put you in that special class of people who never have to worry about money for the rest of their lives. Only a few of us ever have this opportunity. You'd be foolish to let it go by without making the most of it.

Not that you'll probably be a millionaire overnight. How long it takes depends on your course of action. The options are open. You may buy into a going business, start from scratch, go public or simply branch out from your present base. All in all, the best bet is to go where the opportunities are brightest—where the risks are low and the percentages are in your favor. With a little luck, hard work and imagination you could be in the big money circles in six months, a year or five years. There's no need to rush. Odds are you'll be getting richer and richer as you go along.

Dwight A. didn't need much time to plan the route to his first million. He'd been tossing it around in his mind ever since the

day he cut the ribbon on his first furniture store in downtown
Chicago. After years of selling for others, he used the Pyramid
approach to acquire enough money to set off on his own. The
store he opened proved to be a money machine from the start.

One of the first in the area selling unpainted furniture, Dwight's
outlet tapped a huge and growing market. Millions of consumers, especially young-marrieds on a budget, are out to beat
the high cost of finished furniture. Inflation has pushed prices
through the roof—well beyond the means of low- to middle-
income families with simple tastes. These people have flocked to
Dwight's to pick up high-quality merchandise at savings of from
40 to 50 percent.

In less than two years this brisk business pushed sales to more
than $400,000 annually. And Dwight himself managed to
bankroll over $62,000 for his personal account. For a man who
previously earned about $16,000 a year as a salesman, having
this kind of money in the bank was like a dream come true.

He knew just what to do with it—expand! In dozens of suburban
communities surrounding Chicago's inner city, young couples
were buying up thousands of spanking new condominiums as
fast as they were built. To Dwight, all those new homes and
apartments meant one thing—a lot of empty rooms in need of
furniture. And he wanted to be on the spot to service this
lucrative market.

So Dwight moved to expand his business horizontally. Put
simply, this means buying out the competition. He set his sights
on several furniture dealers already established in promising
suburban communities. For one reason or another, all were in
financial trouble. Dwight learned, through the grapevine, that
they were willing to sell out at bargain prices. They had all
misjudged the consumer preference for inexpensive merchandise

and were now having difficulty moving enough goods to stay in business. Dwight knew that his budget-priced line, combined with his expertise in the field, would succeed where the others failed. So he started buying up competitors one by one.

Horizontal expansion offers excellent opportunities for entrepreneurs with a system. A system for running certain types of business better than anyone else. A system for turning losers into winners—troubled companies into money-makers.

If experience shows that you can do just this, then horizontal expansion is made for you. It means you can profit handsomely by gobbling up and turning around companies others are eager to sell. Sometimes all it takes is a new twist—a unique approach—to change a sleeping dog into a roaring lion.

Take Dwight for example. He wasted no time putting his personal stamp on each new acquisition. The day he acquired title, crack crews moved through each new store, ripping out the old fixtures and replacing them with bright, modern decor. All the heavy, expensive merchandise stocked by the former owners was shipped out to make room for fresh stocks of unpainted furniture priced just right for the areas' young consumers.

And Dwight recognized the importance of two key aspects of horizontal expansion—personnel and promotion. First, to be sure that only top managers ran his branch outlets, he chose those who had first worked with him in the main store. The policy was clear: All field supervisors had to work under Dwight's watchful eyes before running a store of their own. This guaranteed that all key personnel dealing with the public were familiar with the company's sales techniques, operating systems and consumer policies. The importance of this measure cannot be over-emphasized. Poor branch management has caused the downfall of thousands of promising business ventures.

Second, Dwight kicked off each grand reopening with a local advertising blitz designed to establish the stores' new image—to change the former prestige appeal to a hard-hitting campaign stressing budget prices, sales and promotions. Dwight knew instinctively that he'd have to give consumers a good reason to shop in stores they'd previously avoided. They would have to know that unpainted furniture was now in town and that it was the best thing that could happen to the family budget. So he told them. He backed each opening with $5,000 in radio and television advertising in the first month alone.

The system worked like a charm. Dwight acquired his first branch outlet in May, a second in September and two more the following summer. In time, he earned a top reputation throughout the midwest, and prospective sellers approached him daily. He had his pick of the most promising furniture outlets and bought them up in quick succession. In four and a half years he had 21 stores flourishing beautifully across a five-state area. (One unsuccessful unit was sold off at a small loss, and another was liquidated.)

At this time, the business was generating $3 million annually— and growing. Dwight personally drew a salary of $100,000 and a bonus of more than double that. He owned a luxury cooperative apartment close to the main office in downtown Chicago, a 16-room Tudor mansion in suburban Highland Park, a 22-foot sloop and two championship Irish Setters. In more ways than one, Dwight had arrived at the winner's circle.

Buying out competitors may not be your cup of tea. You want to expand, but in new directions. You like your business, but you're ready for new challenges—new fields to conquer. What's more, competitors may be doing just as well as you and are unwilling to sell out for less than exorbitant sums.

If so, you may turn to another proven strategy for business growth—vertical expansion. This approach involves your entry into new types of commercial activities.

Let's say, for example, that you are a small manufacturer of decorative lamps. You buy the component parts from suppliers and assemble the units into finished products. By expanding vertically, you may produce some of your own parts—such as lamp shades or bases. This eliminates some suppliers, reduces costs and boosts profits. In addition, marketing your shades or bases to other assemblers may double or triple your previous sales.

Vertical expansion has many pluses in its favor. Like horizontal expansion, it lets you retain your main business as a foundation for future growth. Since you're still working in the field you know best, your expertise can be put to good use.

What's more, the profit potential is staggering. Vertical expansion can stretch from one end of the business pipeline to the other, combining everything from raw materials processing to retail sales in a single company. You may preside over a fully integrated giant which, just like the oil companies, makes big money producing, transporting and selling its products.

A giant is the only way to describe the company Burt F. built for himself. Two years after his first Pyramid Investment, Burt found himself owning and operating a thriving auto accessories distributorship in Houston, Texas. His initial expense of $412 for an inventory of used batteries quickly blossomed into a sizable business generating annual sales of $310,000.

Loyal to the Pyramid method, Burt bankrolled enough cash to parlay this success to even greater heights. Long aware that his customers—the auto service shops—were making money hand over fist, he yearned to get a piece of the retail action too. By distributing to his own stores as well as to others, Burt knew he could expand his business to ten times its present size. That's the kind of vertical expansion he liked.

So he pooled his money with a sizable bank loan and opened four new retail shops—one in each corner of the city. All of them reflected the very latest thinking in modern merchandising—plenty of floor space, bright and accessible displays, shelf-talkers for impulse sales, heavy advertising, in-store promotions and liberal evening hours. Compared to the usual dark and dusty accessory stores, Burt's Motoramas were fun to shop in.

The public agreed. All four stores experienced heavy traffic six days a week and were filled to capacity nights and Saturdays. By the end of the first year, the Motoramas were posting annual sales of more than $500,000 each—more than $2 million combined. It didn't take long for this end of the business to outproduce the distributorship, which alone was pulling in $1.3 million per year.

But that's only half the story. Success breeds success, and Burt knew it. So he did what every wise business owner should do—he used his ever-expanding influence to wheel and deal for the most lucrative arrangements in the auto accessories business.

Like forcing a giant tire manufacturer to grant him exclusive distribution rights on the best-selling radials in the nation. While the others were fighting each other for the rights to the new tire, Burt pulled out his trump card. As the only distributor in Texas with retail outlets to boot, he could guarantee impressive sales from the start. What's more, he threatened not to stock the new radials in any Motorama stores unless he won the distribution rights.

The argument prevailed. The manufacturer gave in, and Burt signed his name to the most lucrative contract of his life. In 16 months he sold 150,000 radials at an average profit of $15 each. The total take was six and a quarter million dollars. News of this phenomenal success soon reached the highest circles, and Burt was literally inundated with exclusive offers on everything from spark plugs to seat covers. He chose carefully, selecting only the leading products and driving a hard bargain on prices and terms.

There's a lesson here for the inexperienced entrepreneur making a first stab at vertical expansion. That is, use not only the money but also the power you accumulate as a business tool. A tool to get your foot in new markets and to extract the best terms from those who rely on your services.

Vertical expansion can take guts and determination. The reason is simple—the more powerful you become, the more competitors will try to fight you off. Just try entering a new line of business, and you'll see. The established forces may even combine their resources to keep you out.

That's why it's crucial to act only from a position of power. If you have the key to the market, no one can beat you. No one can keep you down. As we've seen, the distributor with the most market power gets the distribution rights too. It works that way almost every time—in almost every type of business.

Burt's no-nonsense strategy never failed to pay off for him. With every successful venture, he wedged his way into new and ever more profitable directions. He used cash, power and influence to build a fully integrated empire that in time was manufacturing auto fog lights in Utah and cassette players in Denver, distributing tires and motor oil throughout the midwest and running 11 accessory shops in Texas and Oklahoma. The annual gross for Burt's Auto Enterprises: $12,430,000.

Today, Burt is a wealthy man. Wealthy enough to turn over the reins of his business to his son while he himself luxuriates on a 15-acre spread in sunny Scotsdale, Arizona. But he still serves as a $120,000 a year advisor to the firm and uses this position to hit home on the two strategies he credits for all of his success: Pyramid Investing and vertical expansion.

When it comes to getting super-rich—and super-famous—nothing matches the open-ended opportunities of the securities markets. Hundreds of shrewd investors have recognized this and have used the market mechanism to amass astounding fortunes in record-breaking time.

When it works, it's the easiest way to make millions. For the market—in spite of all its studied sophistication—is really a gambling institution. Come up with a good bet—a hot new idea—and investors will beat a path to your door for a piece of the action. If that good bet is a company you own, the price of your stock can make you a millionaire overnight.

It happens all the time. All you have to do to try is take your company public in a period when the markets are hot and investors are eager for speculative action. Many who have done exactly this have shot from relative obscurity to the heights of American industry in a year or two.

Take the case of a well-known computer salesman. Prevented by corporate personnel policies from achieving his true potential, he struck out on his own. He developed a unique computer service and formed a small company to market it.

The venture met with instant success. Customers lined up around the country; profits were poured back into the business to achieve even greater growth; and the company was soon ready for listing on a major stock exchange. That final step made the former salesman the first new American billionaire in decades. He is, today, one of our best-known business leaders.

You may want to try for the same results—and you can. Now that you've built up a good-sized business, taking it public may be the best way to parlay what you have into millions. To do it right, you'll need a profitable company with promising prospects and about $50,000 for legal fees and investor relations.

Put simply, going public means opening your company to outside investors. This is done by issuing shares of stock in the firm and letting the shares trade on the open market. Although the process is often associated with large industrial corporations, you can take part in it too.

Before you do anything, however, it is best to discuss all of the angles with a lawyer specializing in securities law. These professionals are best-suited to tell if public ownership makes sense for you. There's no sense jumping into this if the experts counsel against it.

What's more, you'll need help meeting the legal requirements if you decide to go ahead. All public offerings are carefully regulated by the Securities and Exchange Commission (SEC), so you'll want to make sure that you do everything right.

The first step is to file all vital information concerning the offering with the SEC. If your offering is small enough in terms of the amount of stock involved, you may get away with a Regulation A Exemption. This is a simplified registration processed through regional SEC offices. It requires less legal preparation than standard offerings.

Larger offerings must be filed with the SEC headquarters office in Washington, D.C. You'll have to submit a full legal registration package, including a perspective on the stock. Among other things, SEC officials will want a full description of your company, the name of the underwriter, the names and experience of top company managers, executive salaries and the company's by-laws. You will also have to pay a fee based on the value of the offering.

Although the legal requirements may be a headache, don't let them get to you. Remember, going public may make you very wealthy very quickly. Selling the company's stock may bring in up to millions of dollars of fresh capital. That's hard cash to build your business—to expand and improve it and make it grow faster than you ever imagined.

Most important, however, going public creates an established market for your stock. As the shares you own rise in value, so too does your personal fortune. And here's where you can really make a killing. If your stock becomes a hot number with investors, you can sit back and watch your fortune grow to 50 or 100 times its present size. It's all very simple. The higher investors bid up the value of your shares, the more you're worth.

Arnold and Joan K. saw their dreams come true when they took their company PeopleSystems public in 1975. Founded by the couple ten years earlier as a small personnel agency, the firm gradually evolved as an innovative service in the employment field. Rather than recruiting individuals for specific jobs, PeopleSystems put together mini-work-forces for corporate clients. Let's say a major TV network needed a staff of accountants for a special auditing project. PeopleSystems screened the applicants, assembled the group and earned a handsome fee for its efforts.

The concept proved to be extremely popular, and Arnold and Joan opened up branch offices in major cities to handle the business. But their master plan, to establish a nationwide system of 200 offices, required money—big money. So they took the company public, issuing one million shares at $5 each and keeping a quarter million shares for themselves.

And they made one very wise move. Rather than waiting for Wall Street to discover the merits of their stock, they hired a financial public relations firm to tout the appeal of PeopleSystems. The PR people held press conferences, met with financial analysts and prepared attractive reports on the company's past performance.

Investors liked what they heard. They liked the company's consistent growth pattern, low debt, blue chip clientele and proven management. And they started buying—cleaning out the initial offering and pushing the price up to $10 a share in a matter of months.

Then lightning struck. A highly regarded investment service put the stock on its buy list, recommending it to investors looking to make big money on a speculative issue. The race was on. Everyone, it seemed, wanted shares of PeopleSystems—and the price of the shares went through the roof.

A month after it made the buy list, the stock was up to $16 a share. Three weeks later it was $20 a share. Then more good news. An article in the *Wall Street Journal* called the stock "the most promising new issue of the year." By June, PeopleSystems was selling for $23 a share.

For Arnold and Joan, their greatest hopes were now reality. The couple's joint holdings made them millionaires—many times over. Soon after the stock hit its high, they sold their shares, purchased a 17th century villa on the French Riviera and spent their days sailing a yacht on the warm Mediterranean. They drew down heavy fees for advisory work but visited the company only once a year for board meetings.

They were rich, famous and carefree. That, in a nutshell, is the power of the market.

Money also brings mobility. The freedom to invest wherever you like—whenever you like. There's no need to stay in your present field at all. Sell off, liquidate or simply close up shop—and use the proceeds to buy into something else.

Shop around for that one opportunity you know will make it big. As a potential partner with more than $50,000 to invest, you'll be in demand—sought after by scores of entrepreneurs with good ideas for making money. Take your time. Pick the best. Put your money in one new business or in ten. If you play your cards right, you'll make a fortune in each.

You can let it be known you're in the market for business proposals by placing a "Capital to Invest" ad in the *Wall Street Journal, Fortune* magazine or local financial publications. Or you can register with the scores of business brokers operating in all major cities. These brokers specialize in bringing together business interests. They can put you in touch with other entrepreneurs looking for investment partners or can recommend promising companies up for sale in your price range. You'll find brokers listed in the yellow pages or in business papers.

Now that you've made your mark, you may even want to put your money to work backing others. A novice entrepreneur starting out with a good idea but with little money, for example, may present just the opportunity you're looking for. Let's say it's a woman inventor with designs for a revolutionary hair dryer that works twice as fast as existing models. Backing her invention from the start can yield you millions if the product proves successful. That's exactly how the big money boys—the venture capitalists—turn limited investments into financial bonanzas. Now you can too! You've made it—so start thinking big!

"The Pyramid system worked wonders for me," says Kurt G. of Minneapolis, Minn. "By age 35 I'd parlayed a starting investment of $190 for an office building coffee service into a lump sum cash account of $73,000. Of course, I'd been through three progressively larger businesses in the meantime, and I was ready to make the really big move of my life. I never dreamed I would have over $70,000 to invest, and when I did I wanted to make the most of it. No business I had been involved in up to that date had enough potential, so I looked elsewhere to invest my money."

He decided to "shotgun" his profits across a broad range of business interests. He put $15,000 into an ice cream franchise outlet and hired local college kids to run it, sank $15,000 into backing the prototype production of an electronic teaching aid, bought a $25,000 silent partnership in a men's clothing store, and dropped another $15,000 into short-term food importing deals.

"After working for others for so much of my life, I wanted to make sure I was never again dependent on a single source of income," Kurt says. "So I planted my money in a lot of different gardens. I knew that if one investment went sour, the others would keep on producing. What's more, I had the chance of making it big with each one of them."

And big he made it. Kurt's strategy proved to be brilliant. Some of the money was put in long-term ventures; others in short. Some were speculative investments; others extremely prudent. Each paid off well, producing both handsome capital gains and steady income. As a result, Kurt had achieved his objective—he was set for life.

The ice cream shop—the first store in a newly opened mall—proved to be a gold mine. The mall was a hit with local consumers and drew heavy traffic 12 hours a day, every day. Kurt's cut, after he wrote off all salary and related expenses, was $36,000 per year and rising. The original $15,000 investment had grown in value to more than $200,000.

After initial production difficulties, the electronic teaching aid proved to be the breakthrough its backers had hoped for. The prototype model received wide critical acclaim and a *Fortune* 500 manufacturer made a bid for the rights. Kurt sold out his share for $350,000 cash, $110,000 worth of the corporation's stock and royalties of one-half percent per year for a decade. Stock dividends and royalties produced a monthly income of $56,000.

The men's clothing store—soon the largest in the state—grew into a major chain with four suburban branches. Kurt's interest is now valued at close to a quarter of a million dollars, and his annual bonus from the business ranges between $50,000 and $65,000.

The food importing venture—the final investment—has never made much money. "But it's the kind of challenge I like best," Kurt notes, "so I devote most of my time to it. I'm a wealthy man now. I can afford to do what pleases me.

"As far as I'm concerned, my experience shows that you can cut your risks and pad your profits by getting involved in a number of business interests simultaneously. My advice on how to do it? Study your moves—be thorough—and you can make millions. It's a first-class strategy for growth."

Thanks Kurt. We agree.

INVESTING AND PROTECTING
YOUR FIRST MILLION:
Case Histories
for the Wealthy Investor

8

Congratulations. You have reached the pinnacle. You are now a full-fledged member of the world's most exclusive club—the one only millionaires can join.

You have wealth, power, leisure and influence. You are known in the richest circles, and your presence is welcome there. You are on a first-name basis with industrialists, politicians and celebrities. You have land, homes, yachts, custom clothes and a reserved seat in the finest dining rooms in town. And most important, you have millions in stocks, bonds and cash.

So the question is, where do you go from here? Now that your wildest dreams are reality, what next? What do you do for an encore? Well, the answer is really up to you.

The options are many. You can sit back and enjoy the good life, putting the bulk of your fortune in safe, steady investments like bonds or blue chip stocks. You can spend it all on personal luxuries like diamonds, jet planes, great art and sculpture. Or you can make the so-called Super Investments the very rich have been making for years. The kind of investments for which you need a million dollars or more just to get started.

Super Investments are more than just extraordinary gambles. They are the kind of super deals that make it so nice to be rich. Why? Because Super Investments help the wealthy achieve all major investment objectives simultaneously. You can live to the hilt, protect your fortune and reap fabulous profits all at once.

Just what are these Super Investments? In most cases, they are special opportunities made possible by little-known tax provisions or investment techniques. They help you make or protect your earnings in a way the small investor can never hope to do.

Investing in motion picture production is a good example. More than 15 percent of all major movies are now financed in full or in part by independent investors. Many have been hit films like *Shampoo, Funny Lady* and *Taxi Driver.*

Investing in the "silver screen" offers more than just glamour. A lot more. It offers a superlative way to rake in hefty profits. Profits of double, triple or four times your original stake in less than a year.

This is no place for the average wage earner. Only successful Pyramid Investors or other members of the moneyed classes can participate. After all, many deals of this kind require a million dollars or more up front just to get a piece of the action.

And action there is. So when Carol F. of Chappaqua, N.Y. went shopping for a suitable investment for the $2.3 million she'd made selling beauty courses—she turned to the "film biz."

It was a wise choice. A well-known investment advisor specializing in the film industry arranged Carol's first motion picture deal. Investing $1,050,000 of Carol's money, the adviser set up a so-called "amortization purchase." That's a special deal enabling Pyramid Investors like Carol to buy a completed movie with a small down payment of only 25 percent of the actual price. The beauty of the deal is this: investors can then deduct depreciation for the film based on its full price. A small down payment, therefore, can produce a healthy tax deduction.

Carol's million-dollar-plus investment was sufficient for her to conclude the amortization purchase on her own. She bought the full rights to an epic film, *The Violent Sky*—a movie with a strong dramatic story and an all-star cast.

Film deals are Super Investments, because there is a good chance of multiplying the initial investment several times over within a short period of time. *The Violent Sky*, for example, satisfied the public's craving for entertaining family pictures. As a result, it was a box office hit from the very first screening, winding up as *Variety* magazine's sixth biggest money-maker of the year. Carol's profit was $5.1 million.

The opportunities are ripe to buy into all types of films. Production funds are scarce, and many of the studios are eager for outside capital. That means you can pick and choose among a wide variety of film ventures from low-budget specialty pictures to star-studded extravaganzas. In a typical year, wealthy investors sink more than $100 million into all types of films. You can be one of them.

Amortization purchases are not the only way to buy into the film business. You can also grab a piece of the action by taking part in one of the many "production service companies" now in operation. These are limited partnerships set up solely to produce and finance films.

Investors put up only about 25 percent of a film's production costs and borrow the rest from a bank as a non-recourse loan. This means the debt is charged against box office receipts and there is no recourse against the individual investors. (That's the kind of financial protection Super Investments offer.)

Just as in amortization purchases, investors in production service companies can deduct the amount "at risk" in the film venture. You are entitled to deduct your share of the full production costs of the film during the year in which the investment is made.

You can explore the whole area of film investments by touching base with so-called "film packagers." These investment advisors specialize in motion picture financing. They will help you choose an ideal film investment and will provide you with a list of properties available for financing.

Film packagers are based in New York, Los Angeles and Chicago. You can contact them by checking with your bankers, checking with the major movie studios or by placing a "capital to invest" ad in the *Wall Street Journal*. Make sure the advisor you deal with has a good track record and be sure to consult with your accountant or attorney before signing.

Although motion pictures offer a fast return on your money, other Super Investments are geared towards long-term returns. These extended investments seek three major objectives: providing a secure outlet for substantial sums of capital, generating significant annual income and multiplying the initial investment by many times its orginal value.

In addition, most long-term Super Investments must be made in growth industries—those businesses likely to experience steadily higher revenues for at least 15 consecutive years. Add to this our other Super Investment criteria, and you have a tall order. Only exceptional opportunities will fill the bill.

One industry which qualifies is rarely considered an industry at all. It is the great pastime of sports—and although it is often thought of as fun and games, it is really big business.

The public's appetite for sports is insatiable. Year after year, more and more people attend an ever-wider spectrum of sporting events. New games like tennis and soccer rise to phenomenal popularity. And the old favorites such as football and baseball continue to rack up record ticket sales and television revenues. People of all ages are watching, listening to and playing sports more than ever before.

Try to think of a national event with wider appeal than the Super Bowl or World Series. What other happening has the power to draw 50 million viewers to their television sets on a Sunday afternoon? Not a Presidential address, a first-run film or an award-winning play. What else would motivate the mass public to spend billions on tickets, racquets, bats, balls, special outfits and uniforms in every size, color and style? Only sports.

You can get a piece of this action by investing in American sports. By putting your money into one of many Super Investments in team ownership, equipment sales, manufacturing or sports promotion. The potential is unlimited if you take the time and care required to select the best opportunities.

Does sports qualify as a growth industry? You bet it does! People have been devoted to sports since early civilization, and this popularity has grown through the centuries. What's more, the industry is now ripe for accelerated expansion. Automation, shorter work weeks and less commuting time are allowing Americans to concentrate on leisure activities. That means more time and money will now be spent on sports.

You can cash in on this boom by making a Super Investment in the sports world. You'll need two things: at least $1 million in investment capital and the Pyramid Investor's knack for finding "the voids that need filling." In other words, you'll have to look around for those lucrative opportunities just waiting for the sharp entrepreneur to discover and develop.

Steer clear of the established and highly competitive markets. Don't even think, for example, of buying an existing baseball franchise. Even if you could find a seller, the costs are too high and the yield too low for Pyramid Investors. Look instead for ventures selling for about $1 million and likely to earn a 300 percent return on your investment within five years.

Search for the new and most promising developments. Like the franchise for a newly established soccer team. Or the rights to a team in a new tennis league. Or the patent for a revolutionary new golf club. These ground-floor opportunities offer reasonable buy-in terms and exceptional pay-back potential.

Remember, sports is a fast-paced business where tastes change overnight and fortunes can be made just as fast. Think of the popularity of the metal tennis racket. For generations wood racquets dominated the game—metal racquets were hardly ever seen, much less used, in championship play. Then suddenly—as if its time had come—the use of metal racquets spread like the popularity of tennis itself. Millions of men and women switched from the standard wood equipment to steel and aluminum models. As expected, manufacturers in on the boom from the start cleaned up, earning multi-million dollar profits in a single tennis season. And these firms—some of which are small, innovative manufacturers—still dominate the metal racquet market to this day.

When planning a Super Investment in sports or any other field, use the following table to determine whether or not you'll earn enough to make the risk worthwhile:

Investments of $1 million or more should produce earnings of

5 to   15 percent of the invested amount the first year
16 to   20 percent of the invested amount the second year
31 to   40 percent of the invested amount the third year
60 to   83 percent of the invested amount the fourth year
175 to 350 percent of the invested amount the fifth year

You can gauge the yield on a projected investment by doing some market research into the amount of business you are likely to experience. This information can be pieced together by using census data, commerce department statistics and special trade reports. (The basics of market research are discussed in Chapter 1.)

Reggie B.'s Super Investment in a new midwest hockey league franchise surpassed even his most optimistic expectations. A fabulously successful Pyramid Investor, Reggie had already amassed a personal fortune of $3.9 million through a fried chicken chain he'd built from scratch in his home town of Gary, Indiana.

When he learned that a new league was accepting franchise bids in a neighboring state, Reggie moved fast to seize the opportunity. He knew that of all major spectator sports hockey was among the fastest growing, chalking up attendance gains year after year. That's the kind of action he knew he could bank on.

Big league sports investing, however, is open only to big league investors—those with lots of cash to put up front. In this case, bidding for the franchise reached $2.9 million. Although hesitant to invest such a sizable sum single-handedly, Reggie bit the bullet, wrote out a check and signed on the dotted line. He now owned a hockey team.

And it was a nice thing to own, especially when the money started rolling in—which did not take long. Three weeks after the signing—before the team had ever hit the ice—Reggie sealed a three year deal granting exclusive television rights to station KPP-TV. The net price was $3.2 million. Reggie's investment was fully repaid—plus a $300,000 profit—before a single hockey ticket was sold. That's a Super Investment.

And the money-machine was just starting to produce. The home fans supported Reggie's skaters like the old Brooklyn Dodger fans of the 1940's. Every game was a sellout—the 33,100 seat arena filled to capacity. Season tickets were sold out opening day, and all the rest were gobbled up soon after. It was a seller's market, and Reggie raked in the cash left and right. He struck it rich as a Pyramid Investor.

Let's take a close look at Reggie's earnings:

Annual ticket sales: $5,296,000
Annual television rights: $1,075,000
Annual radio rights: $200,000
Annual receipts from stadium concessions: $2,078,324
Annual promotional licensing deals: $741,000

Total annual receipts: $9,390,324
Total annual expenses: $5,089,570
Annual profit: $4,300,754

So Reggie's personal profit in the early years of the franchise exceeded $4.3 million annually. The money rolled in faster than he could spend it; the team brought him fame, glory and a divisional championship; and he had enough free time to idle the summers in a 25-room town house he'd built on the Rive Gauche in Paris.

And he could travel abroad with a free mind. His money was invested in a growth industry, generating higher profits and revenue year in and year out. The nation's love of sports made him very wealthy—and he was getting richer every day. Reggie had found his Super Investment. He could live in splendor for the rest of his days.

So can you. All you have to do is make a wise choice for that final Pyramid Investment of $1 million or more. An investment that will grow and protect your fortune at the same time.

Like the investment Dave R. made with the sizable sum he'd amassed selling wide-width women's shoes by mail. Starting out with only $400 and a good idea, Dave parlayed his stake into an ever-larger mail order venture. Called ShoeFinders, the company struck a chord with women who needed the extra-wide shoe sizes most stores never stock. To meet their needs, thousands shopped by mail, and most did business with Dave.

That's why six years after its founding ShoeFinders was the biggest company of its kind in the nation. The firm employed 71 people, sold 200,000 pairs of shoes per year and generated annual sales of more than $5 million. By the time the business was ripe enough to be sold, Dave was ready to snare the highest possible price and move on to something even bigger. So he sold ShoeFinders for $9 million, collecting a personal profit of more than $4 million. For a man who had made only $175 a week in a department store six years earlier, the rise to the millionaire class was a wonderful personal triumph. A triumph for Dave and for Pyramid Investing.

Dave's next step was to fulfill a life-long dream. To take the one step he'd thought about over and over for years. Now he was ready to act.

For as long as Dave could remember, only one group of business people made money all the time—bankers. Only this one group seemed to make money—big money—through thick and thin, through good and bad times. Dave wanted a piece of that action. He was shooting for the top—and he knew it.

Although starting a bank involved more red tape than Dave had a mind for, he wanted to function the way bankers do. He wanted to make money simply by lending out his own money for use by others. To let his money do all the work.

Sure enough, he hit on a way. Dave earned all the profits of a banker—without most of the bother—by becoming a *Commercial Factor*. He cleared the way with government officials, secured all the necessary papers and started a factoring service.

What are commercial factors? What do they do? Put simply, factors lend money to other businessmen. Factors provide a popular and critical service, advancing money to companies on the basis of their accounts receivable.

Let's say Company ABC, for example, is the kind of business that needs cash on hand at all times. Management must collect on its bills as soon as possible so there will be funds available to buy new merchandise, equipment or supplies.

If ABC's customers are slow payers, however, management is in a bind. No cash means no money to purchase inventories or to keep the company functioning smoothly. That can mean big trouble, especially in volatile industries like apparel manufacturing and auto sales.

There is, however, a solution to the slow-payment syndrome—*Commercial Factoring*. Factors assume the worry and expense of late payments, enabling client companies like ABC to operate without interruption.

Rather than waiting out slow-paying accounts, for example, ABC's management simply turns over all invoices directly to a factor. The factor, in turn, immediately reimburses ABC for up to 80 percent of the invoice values. The remaining balance is settled by the factor when the account is actually paid.

What's in it for the factor? How does he make a banker's profits? By providing this credit service to companies like ABC, factors earn up to 10 percent on all cash advances plus an additional service fee ranging from 1 to 2 ½ percent of turnover. You make big money—at times very big money—simply by lending money. What could be easier?

And the beauty of factoring is that the loans you make are secured. Your risks are low because you take control of customer companies' accounts receivable. You make money simply by lending funds on a short-term basis.

That's exactly the way it worked for Dave's factoring service. His company—called International Factors Ltd.—solicited customers by placing a small ad (cost: $775) in the *Wall Street Journal.* The response was overwhelming—331 companies expressed a strong interest in doing business with International Factors.

The next step involved selecting the most credit worthy respondents. Dave hired a credit agency to do the research and was soon presented with a list of 31 companies with top credit records. All were financially sound outfits doing business in stable industries. That's the kind of credit risk a factor can bank on.

During the first six months of operation, Dave met with prospective customers at their places of business. He used this opportunity to take a close look at all the prospects and to explain his fee schedule in detail. For the most part, the meetings proved extremely productive. Twenty-nine companies signed on as full-time customers with International Factors.

Cash started rolling in almost immediately. Dave leased a suite of offices in downtown Chicago, hired a staff of accountants and credit specialists and worked out a financial arrangement with a group of three local banks.

By the company's second anniversary, it was established as a major factoring firm—one of the largest independents in the midwest. In a typical month, International Factors advanced loans of roughly $8 million to a group of more than 40 key customers. In return, International Factors earned an average of $1,300,000 in interest on these transactions. And thanks to tight credit policies, bad debts were kept to less than one percent of this total.

As International Factors' principle stockholder, Dave's personal share of the take approached $2.3 million per year. In a few years, he salted away enough cash to live out the rest of his days in carefree splendor.

He hired a full-time operating executive to run the business day to day, purchased a custom-built 101-foot luxury houseboat and retired to a life of leisure in the waters around Hawaii. A staff of nine served Dave and his wife on the boat, and they came to shore only once a week for a game of tennis with local friends.

What's more, Dave remained president and chairman of International Factors and continued to rake in millions of dollars a year. The less he did, the wealthier he became—and he loved every minute of it. Dave owed his fortune only to himself. He had only himself to thank for having the foresight and the savvy to put his earnings into a Super Investment—to become a commercial factor.

Dave's investment was more than profitable. It met the test of a true Super Investment by protecting as well as expanding his fortune. When it comes to investing that first million, security is just as important as profit.

Dave enjoyed the best of both worlds. International Factors produced phenomenal profits and, similar to banking, was a business likely to do well regardless of the prevailing economic conditions. Factoring, after all, is a growth business. Money lenders never have to look far for business.

Even recessions, which can play havoc with most traditional businesses, actually help factors earn greater profits than ever. The cash problems caused by recessions prompt more and more companies to turn to factors for financial assistance. That's because when times are bad individuals and corporations put off paying bills for as long as possible. Debtors hold on to past-due funds way beyond the normal payment dates. Companies with many delinquent accounts must turn to factors to keep the cash flowing.

Factoring is one of those rare opportunities reserved exclusively for the very wealthy. You need a lot of chips to play the game, but once you qualify the odds are stacked in your favor. And when it comes to pure earning potential, the sky is the limit.

What, you may ask, happens to all this factoring, sports and other Super Investment income at tax time? Is there a way to legally limit the tax bite and increase the amount of retained earnings? Well—thanks to some beneficial laws and regulations—the answer is yes. Pyramid Investors can have their cake and eat it too.

You can do so by taking advantage of the few remaining tax shelters. (The Tax Reform Act of 1976 has eliminated most multiple write-off tax shelters.) Although we touched on this topic earlier in this chapter, it is important enough to warrant a closer look. For now that you are ready for the million-dollar-plus Pyramid Investment—the Super Investment—you'll want to be sure that some of your high-tax-bracket earnings are legally sheltered. You'll want to keep as much as is legally possible.

How you can put these shelters to work for you is simple enough to explain. Let's, for example, take another look at Dave R.—the man whose Super Investment in commercial factoring produced an annual income of $2.3 million. To keep as much of this income as possible from high taxation, Dave set up a real estate tax shelter.

He put up $100,000 cash for the construction of Glen Brook—a garden apartment development located near Chicago. A local bank granted a $900,000 mortgage to cover the bulk of the $1 million purchase price. So for only $100,000 of his own money, Dave now owned a residential development valued at ten times that amount.

The beauty of this arrangement is made evident by the tax laws. Thanks to a tax provision Dave could take deductions based on the combined amount of the borrowed money plus his own investment. His tax shelter was based primarily on leverage (borrowed funds).

It works like this: Even though Dave put up only $100,000 cash, he could legally depreciate the full amount of the property—one million dollars. Let's say he depreciated the property over 25 years. He would then have an annual depreciation deduction of $40,000. So in only three years' time (3x$40,000=$120,000) his tax deduction exceeded the amount of the original investment. Dave used these deductions to shelter income earned from his interests in International Factors.

Again, the nice thing about it is that he did it with someone else's money—in this case, a bank's money. He used leverage to cut his risks and his tax bills simultaneously.

You can do the same by taking part in real estate syndicates. By taking this approach, you'll be making investments with a group, or so-called syndicate, of investors. The real benefit here is that a professional financial manager will watch over your investment while you devote your attention elsewhere. Speak to your accountant or stockbroker about the benefits of investing in real estate syndicates. Most of the major brokerage firms put together real estate packages you can join.

One more point. Many of the greatest fortunes ever known have been made by buying and selling real estate. So although you may purchase property for tax considerations, you may wind up making a bundle on the appreciation as well. That's the kind of extra bonus that makes for a Super Investment.

Finally, you may want to consider what may well be the most exotic and least-known Super Investment of all. That is, relocating to a tax-free haven. Now that you have earned your stripes as a Pyramid Investor—now that you have amassed your first million—you may well want to reinvest your fortune where there are no income taxes at all.

And believe it or not, such places do exist. Some, in fact, can be lovely places to live and do business. Like Cayman Islands in the warm and sunny Caribbean. This tax-free paradise lets you live surrounded by beauty—without a worry in the world about state, federal or local taxes. For the most part, what you earn is what you keep.

All you have to do is invest your money in a bona fide business venture in any of the world's tax-free havens. (You'll find them listed in Commerce Clearing House publications in the library.) As long as your earnings stay within the tax haven, they are tax free.

"The tax breaks are all they are cracked up to be," says Bill A., a former Nebraskan now relocated at a tax-free island in the Caribbean. "But there's more to it than that. I'm living like an absolute baron here on a picturesque island that's sunny and warm every day. There's no smog, crime or traffic, and even the local leaders are helpful and responsive. You can't beat this way of life."

Everyone agrees that Bill is the richest man on the island—perhaps in this part of the world. A former auto mechanic from Lincoln, Nebraska, he left school at 16 to work in Jen's Speed Shop two blocks from his home. By age 26 he realized he was going nowhere tightening bolts on Fords and Chevies. So he put $489 into his first Pyramid Investment and launched the Station Maintenance Corp.—a service specializing in cleaning gasoline service stations quickly and economically. The initial investment: $285 for a used truck, $115 for hoses and cleaning equipment and $89 for signs and uniforms.

The rest, as they say, is history. Since a clean station attracts customers, station owners across the nation were eager to sign up for Bill's service. It was soon obvious that Bill had "found a void and filled it." News of his company spread, and the firm grew without stopping. In less than three years, 13,000 customers in 31 states were on the books. By the time Bill was 31, Station Maintenance Corp. was generating $5 million per year and climbing.

A firm believer in dealing from power, Bill chose this time to sell his interests in the company. Selling out at a period of peak earnings, Bill believed, would be the best way to make a killing. He was right. Two months after the company was on the market, Bill signed over ownership to a group of Japanese investors. Bill's take for the transaction: $9.6 million.

Now wealthy and independent, Bill wasted no time in tying up his affairs in the U.S. and moving on for good to the lazy little island he'd had his heart set on for years. He threw out his winter clothes, bought the family a lavish tropical wardrobe and chartered a jet for the flight to the sun.

Soon after his arrival, Bill deposited his money in a tax-free bank account, built a 31-room modern mansion on a bluff overlooking a coral lagoon and started the ball rolling on a grand new business venture right on the island.

From the day he first visited the island as a summer tourist, Bill recognized its potential as an international vacation spot. A perfect place for the beautiful people to sun, swim, party, play tennis and disco. The weather was majestic, the beaches pink and the water warm and shimmering in the tropical sun. The elements were ideal—just waiting for a hip investor to put up the kind of chic restaurants and resorts to attract the big-spending jet setters.

Now Bill had the money and the smarts—and he was ready to pour in millions to develop the island according to his master

178 Investing and Protecting Your First Million

plan. That meant creating Alenda—the ultimate luxury spa designed for the wealthiest travelers. The resort was the only one of its kind in the world—a futuristic compound of glass and steel villas featuring 11 swimming pools, motion picture screening rooms, 60-foot sailing yachts, 33 tennis courts and 9 lush dining rooms built on the waterfront. It was custom-made for those who knew the best and expected it wherever they traveled.

Working with a team of French architects and a Dutch bank, Bill developed the resort in 13 months of nonstop work. When Alenda opened its doors to guests on New Year's day, it was filled to capacity and was hailed around the world as a "glass jewel in the Caribbean."

Visitors paid dearly for luxuriating in Alenda's splendid facilities. Rates ranged from $225 per person per day to up to $1,750 for the Island Governor's Suite. Breakfasts averaged $12, lunches $30 and dinner $75 to $80 with wine. The typical weekly bill for a couple in standard facilities approached $5,500.

Alenda's occupancy rate started off at an incredible 88 percent full, climbed into the 90's a month later and never dropped from this peak. Reservations for suites soon stretched out two years in advance, and rooms were hard to come by at any price. In dollars and cents, the figures were incredible. Alenda's 489 guest rooms were generating more than $140 million annually.

Obviously, Bill's Super Investment paid off extravagantly. He had turned a $3 million investment (coupled with bank financing) into a major business enterprise employing, 1,980 workers. What's more, this uneducated former auto mechanic achieved an incredible goal—thanks to profits from Alenda he was now earning personal income at the rate of $1 million per month.

"All tax free," Bill reminds us. "Not only could I save and spend all I made as I chose, but I could also leave the remaining fortune to my children.

"I've made more money than I could possibly spend, and if I had to start all over again I could do it once more. Making the kind of fortune I've made is uncommon—but certainly not impossible. All you have to do is have the courage to make that first small investment—no more than a couple of hundred dollars—and then nurse it along. When the business is nice and ripe, sell it off and buy bigger. You'll get to the top before you know it. Just look for the right angles—go against the crowds—and you too can make it.

"Once you get the hang of it, you feel you can do anything. And it's true. A good Pyramid Investor can parlay $50 into $5 million as many times as he has to. If you've never tried it, I suggest you get started today. You'll never get rich by waiting for it to happen."

That's good advice. Expand your present business or start a new one. Look for the right opportunity and take the plunge. You have much to gain.

Remember, you no longer have to dream about getting rich. You can make it happen. Make your first Pyramid Investment now, and you may be spending your earnings that much sooner. Trust in yourself, and you'll see the difference.

Good Luck!

APPENDIX

SBA FIELD OFFICES

I

RO   150 Causeway St., 10th Floor
Boston, Mass. 02114
(617) 223-2100

DO   150 Causeway St., 10th Floor
Boston, Mass. 02114
(617) 223-2100

POD   302 High Street—4th Floor
Holyoke, Mass. 01040
(413) 536-8770

DO   Federal Building, Room 512
40 Western Avenue
Augusta, Maine 04330
(207) 622-6171

DO   55 Pleasant St., Room 213
        Concord, N.H. 03301
        (603) 224-4041

DO   Federal Building, Room 710
        450 Main Street
        Hartford, Conn. 06103
        (203) 244-2000

DO   Federal Building, Room 210
        87 State Street
        Montpelier, Vt. 05602
        (802) 233-7472

DO   57 Eddy Street, Room 710
        Providence, R. I. 02903
        (401) 528-1000

II

RO   26 Federal Plaza, Room 3214
        New York, N.Y. 10007
        (212) 264-1468

DO   26 Federal Plaza, Room 3100
        New York, N.Y. 10007
        (212) 264-4355

POD   131 Jericho Turnpike
        Jericho, Long Island, N.Y. 11753
        (516) 997-7760

DO   Chardon and Bolivia Streets
        Hato Rey, Puerto Rico 00919
        (809) 763-6363

POD   Franklin Building
        St. Thomas, Virgin Islands 00801
        (809) 774-1331

DO   970 Broad Street, Room 1635
Newark, N.J. 07102
(201) 645-3581

POD 1800 East Davis Street
Camden, N.J. 08104
(609) 757-5183

DO   Federal Building, Room 1073-100
South Clinton Street
Syracuse, N.Y. 13202
(315) 473-3350

BO   Federal Building, Room 1311
111 West Huron Street
Buffalo, N.Y. 14202
(716) 842-3240

BO   180 State Street, Room 412
Elmira, N.Y. 14904
(607) 734-1571

POD 99 Washington Avenue
Twin Towers Bldg., Room 922
Albany, N.Y. 12210
(518) 472-4411

POD Federal Building
100 State Street
Rochester, N.Y. 14604
(716) 263-5700

III

RO   1 Bala Cynwyd Plaza, Suite 646 West Lobby
231 St. Asaphs Rd.
Philadelphia, Bala Cynwyd, Pa. 19004
(215) 597-3311

DO   1 Bala Cynwyd Plaza, Suite 400 East Lobby
231 St. Asaphs Rd.
Philadelphia, Bala Cynwyd, Pa. 19004
(215) 597-3311

BO   1500 North 2nd Street
Harrisburg, Pa. 17108
(717) 782-2200

BO   Penn Place
20 N. Pennsylvania Avenue
Wilkes-Barre, Pa. 18702
(717) 825-6811

BO   Federal Building, Room 5207—Lockbox 16
844 King Street
Wilmington, Del. 19801
(302) 571-6294

DO   7800 York Road
Baltimore, Towson Md. 21204
(301) 962-2150

DO   Lowndes Building
109 North 3rd St., Room 301
Clarksburg, W. Va. 26301
(304) 623-3461

BO   Charleston National Plaza, Suite 628
Charleston, W. Va. 25301
(304) 343-6181

DO   Federal Building, Room 1401
1000 Liberty Avenue
Pittsburgh, Pa. 15222
(412) 644-2780

DO   Federal Building, Room 3015
400 North 8th Street

Richmond, Va. 23240
(804) 782-2617

DO   1030 15th St. N.W.—Suite 250
Washington, D.C. 20417
(202) 655-4000

IV

RO   1401 Peachtree St., N.E. Room 470
Atlanta, Ga. 30309
(404) 526-0111

DO   1720 Peachtree Street, N.E.
Atlanta, Ga. 30309
(404) 526-0111

DO   908 South 20th Street, Room 202
Birmingham, Ala. 35205
(205) 254-1000

DO   230 S. Tryon Street
Charlotte, N.C. 28202
(704) 372-0711

POD   215 South Evans Street
Greenville, N.C. 27834
(919) 752-3798

DO   1801 Assembly Street, Room 117
Columbia, S. C. 29201
(803) 765-5376

DO   Petroleum Bldg., Suite 690
200 E. Pascagoula Street
Jackson, Miss. 39201
(601) 969-4371

BO   Gulf Nat. Life Insurance Bldg., 2nd Floor
111 Fred Haise Blvd.

Biloxi, Miss. 39530
(601) 863-1972

DO   Federal Building, Room 261
400 West Bay St., P.O. Box 3507
Jacksonville, Fla. 32202
(904) 791-2011

DO   Federal Building, Room 188
600 Federal Pl.
Louisville, Ky. 40202
(502) 582-5971

DO   222 Ponce De Leon Blvd., 5th Floor
Miami, Coral Gables, Fla. 33184
(305) 350-5011

POD 1802 N. Trask Street, Suite 203
Tampa, Fla. 33607
(813) 288-2594

DO   404 James Robertson Parkway, Suite 1012
Nashville, Tenn. 37219
(615) 749-5022

BO   Fidelity Bankers Building
502 South Gay Street, Room 307
Knoxville, Tenn. 37902
(615) 637-9300

POD Federal Building, Room 211
167 North Main Street
Memphis, Tenn. 38103
(901) 521-3588

V

RO   Federal Building, Room 838
219 South Dearborn Street

Chicago, Ill. 60604
(312) 353-4400

DO   Federal Building, Room 437
219 South Dearborn Street
Chicago, Ill. 60604
(312) 353-4528

BO   One North, Old State Capital Plaza
Springfield, Ill. 62701
(217) 525-4416

DO   1240 East 9th Street, Room 317
Cleveland, Ohio 44199
(216) 522-4180

DO   34 North High Street, Tonti Bldg.
Columbus, Ohio 43215
(614) 469-6860

BO   Federal Building, 550 Main Street
Cincinnati, Ohio 45202
(513) 684-2814

DO   477 Michigan Avenue, McNamara Building
Detroit, Mich. 48226
(313) 226-6075

BO   Don H. Bottum University Center
540 W. Kaye Avenue
Marquette, Mich. 49855
(906) 225-1108

DO   Century Building
575 North Pennsylvania St., 5th Floor
Indianapolis, Ind. 46204
(317) 269-7272

DO   122 West Washington Avenue, Room 713
Madison, Wis. 53703
(608) 252-5261

BO   735 West Wisconsin Avenue, Room 905
Continental Bank & Trust Co.
Milwaukee, Wis. 53233
(414) 224-3941

POD   500 South Barstow St., Room 16
Federal Off. Bldg. & U.S. Courthouse
Eau Claire, Wis. 54701
(715) 834-9012

DO   12 South 6th Street, Plymouth Building
Minneapolis, Minn. 55402
(612) 725-2362

VI

RO   Regal Park Office Bldg., Suite 230
1720 Regal Row
Dallas, Tex. 75235
(214) 749-1011

DO   1100 Commerce Street, Room 300
Dallas, Tex. 75202
(214) 749-1011

POD   Federal Building
100 South Washington Street
Marshall, Tex. 75670
(214) 935-1411

DO   Patio Plaza Building
5000 Marble Avenue, N.E.
Albuquerque, N. Mex. 87110
(505) 766-5111

DO   One Allen Center
500 Dallas
Houston, Tex. 77002
(713) 226-4011

DO   611 Gaines Street, Suite 900
      Little Rock, Ark. 72201
      (501) 378-5011

DO   712 Federal Office Bldg. & U.S. Courthouse
      1205 Texas Avenue
      Lubbock, Tex. 79408
      (806) 762-7011

BO   4100 Rio Bravo, Suite 300
      El Paso, Tex. 79901
      (915) 543-7200

DO   202 E. Van Buren Street
      Lower Rio Grande Valley
      Harlingen, Tex. 78550
      (512) 423-3011

BO   3105 Leopard Street
      Corpus Christi, Tex. 78408
      (512) 888-3011

DO   Plaza Tower, 17th Floor
      1001 Howard Avenue
      New Orleans, La. 70113
      (504) 589-2611

POD   Fannin Street
      U.S. Post Office & Courthouse Bldg.
      Shreveport, La. 71163
      (318) 226-5196

DO   50 Penn Place, Suite 840
      Oklahoma City, Okla. 73118
      (405) 736-4011

DO   727 E. Durango, Room A-513
      San Antonio, Tex. 78206
      (512) 229-5511

VII

RO   911 Walnut Street, 23rd Floor
        Kansas City, Mo. 64106
        (816) 374-3318

DO   1150 Grande Avenue—5th Floor
        Kansas City, Mo. 64106
        (816) 374-5557

DO   New Federal Building, Room 749
        210 Walnut Street
        Des Moines, Iowa 50309
        (515) 284-4422

DO   Empire State Building
        Nineteen and Farnan Streets
        Omaha, Neb. 68102
        (402) 221-4691

DO   Mercantile Tower, Suite 2500
        One Mercantile Center
        St. Louis, Mo. 63101
        (314) 425-4191

DO   Main Place Building
        110 E. Waterman Street
        Wichita, Kan. 67202
        (316) 267-6566

VIII

RO   Executive Tower Building
        1405 Curtis Street
        Denver, Colo. 80202
        (303) 327-0111

DO   721 19th Street, Room 426A
Denver, Colo. 80202
(303) 327-0111

DO   Federal Building, Room 4001
100 E. B Street
Casper, Wyo. 82601
(307) 328-5330

DO   Federal Building, Room 218
653 2nd Avenue, N.
Fargo, N. Dak. 58102
(701) 783-5771

DO   618 Helena Avenue
Helena, Mont. 59601
(406) 588-6011

DO   Federal Building, Room 2237
125 S. State Street
Salt Lake City, Utah 84111
(801) 588-5500

DO   National Bank Building, Room 402
8th & Main Avenue
Sioux Falls, S. Dak. 57102
(605) 782-4980

BO   Federal Building
515 9th Street
Rapid City, S. Dak. 57701
(605) 782-7000

IX

RO   Federal Building
450 Golden Gate Avenue

Box 36044
San Francisco, Calif. 94102
(415) 556-9000

DO   211 Main Street
       San Francisco, Calif. 94102
       (415) 556-9000

BO   Federal Building, Room 4015
       1130 O. Street
       Fresno, California 93721
       (209) 487-5000

POD   2800 Cottage Way
       Sacramento, Calif. 95825
       (916) 484-4200

DO   301 E. Stewart
       Las Vegas, Nev. 89121
       (702) 385-6011

POD   300 Booth Street
       Reno, Nev. 89504
       (702) 784-5234

DO   1149 Bethal Street, Room 402
       Honolulu, Hawaii 96813
       (808) 546-8950

BO   Ada Plaza Center Building
       Agana, Guam 96910
       (-) 777-8420 (dial operator)

DO   350 S. Figueroa Street, 6th Floor
       Los Angeles, Calif. 90071
       (213) 688-2000

DO   112 N. Central Avenue
Phoenix, Ariz. 85004
(602) 261-3900

DO   Federal Building, Room 4-S-33
880 Front Street
San Diego, Calif. 92188
(714) 293-5444

X

RO   Dexter Horton Bldg., 5th Floor
710 2nd Avenue
Seattle, Wash. 98104
(206) 442-4343

DO   Federal Bldg., Room 1744
915 Second Avenue
Seattle, Wash. 98174
(206) 442-4343

DO   Anchorage Legal Ctr., Suite 200
1016 W. 6th Avenue
Anchorage, Alaska 99501
(907) 272-5561

BO   501 ½ Second Avenue
Fairbanks, Alaska 99701
(907) 452-1951 (dial operator)

DO   216 N. 8th Street, Room 408
Boise, Idaho 83701
(208) 342-2711

DO   Federal Building
1220 S.W. Third Avenue

Portland, Oreg. 97205
(503) 221-2000

DO Court House Building, Room 651
Spokane, Wash. 99210
(509) 452-2100

---

10 Regional Offices (RO)   18 Branch Offices (BO)
63 District Offices (DO)   12 Post-of-Duty (POD)

INDEX

A

Accounts receivable, 170-171
Acid-test ratio, 112
Advertising, 91-92, 147
Amortization purchase, 163
Assets, 74-75

B

Banking, 170-171, 173
Bankruptcy, 43, 83-84, 144
Billionaires, 32
Borrowing, 37
Branch management, 146
Break-even chart, 115
Break-even volume, 113-114
Business basics, 108-109
Business fatigue, 73
Business umbrella, 100
Buying businesses, 54-56, 74-77
Buy signs, 74-77

C

Capital assets, 56
Capital stock, 39
Carnegie, Andrew, 119
Cash reserves, 100-101
Cayman Islands, 175
Census reports, 23-24
    Business Census, 25
    Census Bureau, 26
    Census Bureau Catalog, 26
    Census on Population & Housing,
        24, 104
Commercial factoring, 170-173
Common stock, 152-155
Community referral service, 124-125
Consignment selling, 126-127
Consumer Product Safety Act
        (CPSA), 93
Current ratios, 112
Customer relations, 88-89, 96-97,
        122